When
Christians
DOUBT

Other Books by Don Bridge

When Christians DOUBT

Donald Bridge

A ministry of World Vision

MARC
EUROPE

British Library Cataloguing in Publication Data

Bridge, Donald
    When Christians doubt.
    1. Faith
    I. Title
    248.2   BV4637

    ISBN 0–947697–64–0

Copyright © 1987 by Donald Bridge.
            First published 1987.
            ISBN 0–947697–64–0.
Typeset in Britain for MARC, a division of Kingsway Publications, Lottbridge Drove, Eastbourne, East Sussex BN23 6NT, in Times Roman by Watermark, Hampermill Cottage, Watford WD1 4PL; printed by Acorn Litho Ltd, 634 River Gardens, Feltham, Mx TW14 0RW.

Contents

Dedication

My younger son Paul typed the manuscript of this book during a period when he faced severe, faith-testing problems. His frank questioning and his hurt bewilderment made a contribution to my thinking and added a dimension of stark reality to the issues which this book faces.

Thank you, Paul. I dedicate this book to you with affection.

Donald Bridge
Cleveland

Chapter 1

Faith Asking Questions

A British prime minister once remarked that a week is a long time in politics. The same could be said of a week in the Christian ministry. Almost any week. The kaleidoscope of human situations constantly reshaping before the minister's eyes is the world of human hopes and fears in miniature.

I recall one week, not because it was unusual, but because it was typical. Here are some of the people with whom I had long conversations.

A woman was dying of cancer. She faced the fact that her daughter would be left, still a schoolgirl. Father had long since left home for another woman. We talked calmly of provision that needed to be made and planned which hymns to use at the funeral.

A middle-aged man was painting the block of flats as I left her apartment. He is a well-known atheist in the little town, and he kept me in warm argument for half an hour. Surrounded by paintpots, waving a brush rather dangerously, he explained to me why a recent disastrous earthquake in China proved conclusively that there can be no God worth worshipping, since, he argued, God either could have stopped it but didn't care enough to bother, or wanted to stop it but didn't have the power.

A call later that week took me to an elderly lady stunned by the death of a loved husband. He was 80 when he died. An uninvolved onlooker might well have said that life hardly owed anything to them at that age, and death could scarcely have come as a surprise. But it had. Here were two people with lives intertwined. Marriage had been a true partnership.

They were more like two halves of one person than two separate persons. Now one was left—numbed, silent, lost and disoriented.

The next visit on my list was to a seaman in his middle twenties. Christianity was totally new to him. He had been found by Christ a few weeks previously through the witness of his wife whose own faith was only two months old. The Bible was to them un-explored territory; every religious concept was new. He was reading the Bible, swallowing truth in great undigested gulps and keeping a list of questions to ask me when I called. I could hardly complain that they were peripheral issues. Did God actually make every-thing? Then why did he make cancer and wars and child-murderers? So sin altered the equation...then why did God allow it to? So man has to be free in order to be human and many misuse his freedom...then why did God start the thing at all, since he must have known man would spoil it? And incidentally, who made the Devil?

A church officer visited me next day. She called to confirm once again that an astonishing healing in ans-wer to prayer had 'stuck', so to speak. It was no pas-sing improvement; the patient was off the doctor's list, and the case was closed. In fact it was reported in the *British Medical Journal* (December 1985). The two doctors involved with me in that prayer for heal-ing had become convinced of the reality of miraculous healing of organic disease. But we wondered aloud together. Why healing for her in particular? Why for so few? Why not for the woman with cancer, who had every bit as much faith?

Towards the end of the week I was the fascinated third person in a discussion. An elderly man, some-thing of a war-hero, now felt revolted by the bombing raids he had once led in a far-off war. He was giving all his energy and money to the relief of suffering amongst war-victims of any nationality. He saw it as a repayment to God and to humanity. The motive was deeply religious, but somewhat lacking (dared I suggest it?) in the glorious assurance of God's un-earned love and grace.

In those six incidents, several things strike me as very significant. They all happened within the compass of one week. It was not a particularly unusual week. A clergyman meets many people all the time, and gets to know a great deal more about 'real life' than some folk imagine—as G K Chesterton so wittily points out in his splendid Father Brown detective stories. No, there was nothing unusual about that week and the things I heard. The world is full of people who are agonising, arguing, enquiring, complaining, showing weakness or fortitude or rebellion or patience in the presence of its dark mysteries: the mysteries of pain and sickness, sorrow and bereavement, tragedy and disappointed hopes—the world's hurts.

Second, everyone in the incidents I quote was try-ing to grapple with a question. How could God be re-lated to life's shadows and sorrows? I suppose the fact that I am a clergyman focused the question a bit more sharply. Here, they felt, was a God-slot professional. He ought to know. But I do not believe for one mo-ment that my clerical collar alone was responsible for that. The questions were in their minds anyway. They came out too quickly and easily to be anything but deeply felt. And, in varying response to the different attitudes they showed, I found myself offering de-fence, advice, comfort, explanation, justification, about God. How does religious faith fit into a suffer-ing world? Especially, how does the love and power of God fit in?

I'm almost sure that anyone who makes any effort

to talk about his Christian faith will get very much the
same reaction. 'How *can* you believe in the love of
God when...?' And out come the examples, real
enough, which seem to deny such a faith.

Pain, Experience and Faith

But now comes the most curious thing about my six
incidents. You would have thought that the more
vividly a person is confronted by pain and suffering,
the more impossible he will find it to believe in God.
But it was just the opposite. The woman who faced
the chill certainty of progressive disease was full of
confidence in God. The most important part of our
conversation was when we made it a threesome by
talking to him in prayer. She had known him in the
healthy years, and now her faith, calm and deep-
rooted, gave her confidence in him when the body
wasted and the walls closed in.

On the other hand, my disputatious friend who
claimed to be an atheist knows as little about the *experience* of suffering as he knows about God. The
homeless of China were quite unreal to him, except as
a point to score in an argument. And he is one of those
fortunate people who reach the age of 50 with no pain
in their lives more severe than a twinge of
rheumatism.

The other people stood somewhere between those
two extremes. But the same pattern was apparent. Put
suffering as a theoretical problem, and they were
faced with a poser. Put it in terms of faith—the
willingness to believe—and you saw something quite
different. *Suffering as an experienced fact* (unlike
suffering as an abstract subject for debate) gave depth
and expression to faith.

Put simply and bluntly, pain is a problem to faith,

but it is not a convincing reason for unbelief. It cannot be, for tens of thousands of people who suffer great pain of one kind or another believe in God. People die of cancer, at peace with him. Wives see their husbands snatched from them, and go on serving him. Martyrs die in torment, joyfully calling on him. The Christian gospel is making gains unprecedented in human history in that Third World which has become the epitome of poverty, pain, injustice and sorrow. Many of us find this puzzling. Some find it incredible. But the plain fact is that a suffering world and faith in God's love often go hand in hand. You and I may not know how—but apparently many people do.

Clearing the Path

Religious, experiential, intellectual, emotional—all kinds of difficulties stand in the way of faith. What exactly am I invited to believe? Belief was never meant to be blind credulity. The schoolboy was quite mistaken when he defined faith as 'believing what you know isn't true'. The Bible sets no premium on muddle-headedness and confused thinking. The apostle Peter urges us to 'be prepared to give an answer to everyone who asks you to give the reason for the hope that you have (I Peter 3:15). The apostle Paul was quite prepared to give question-and-answer lectures in a hall in Ephesus designed for that purpose (Acts 19:9). He readily grasped the opportunity to debate his doctrine in the Areopagus in Athens—the Hyde Park Speakers' Corner of the ancient world (Acts 17:16–31), and when he did so he dropped the familiar religious language of his Bible and spoke in the terms of the culture of his hearers—Greek customs, pagan poets and so on.

C S Lewis is the apologist *par excellence* of the twentieth century. Converted with great reluctance from intellectual atheism to Christianity, he could with scintillating ease take on the objections and arguments of his old school of thought, and trounce them thoroughly by presenting the superior claims of simple supernatural biblical Christianity. It is no accident that one of his finest bestsellers is still *The Problem of Pain*.

Apologetics, then, is what some people need: that is, help in understanding the good reasons for believing. The atheistic decorator needed it to silence his objections. The converted seaman needed it to explore his new-found faith. Clearing away the mental undergrowth is one of the great purposes of apologetics. Now, at least, we can see the nature of the path of faith we are invited to pursue.

A lot of the undergrowth is made up of faulty logic, crude sub-Christian ideas of God, and a good deal of confusion about what the Christian is supposed to believe. But apologetics has its limits. C S Lewis admitted that frankly:

> The only purpose (of that particular book) is to solve the intellectual problem raised by suffering. For the far higher task of teaching fortitude and patience I was never fool enough to suppose myself qualified, nor have I anything to offer my readers except my conviction that when pain is to be borne, a little courage helps more than much knowledge, a little human sympathy more than much courage, and the least tincture of the love of God more than all.[1]

Following the Path

What the widow, the sick woman and the war-hero wanted was not clever arguments but clear directions. Their problem was not finding the path through the jungle, but summoning the faith and fortitude to follow it when they found it. For that path takes some disconcerting twists, and it is strewn with sharp stones that hurt the feet. Sometimes it crosses flooded rivers and skirts frightening precipices. Is it really supposed to be as difficult as *this*? Yes it is. The acknowledged Authority on such things, who opened up the way himself, warned us that it is 'small and narrow'. Rather than sorrow, pain and shadow constituting a denial of a God of love, we shall find that they make faith in such a God essential, and find their truest meaning in such a love. That may not be what some of our pop-religious travelling road-shows lead us to expect, but it is what our divine guidebook clearly teaches. While muddled unbelievers say 'a loving God would never let his creatures be hurt', and only slightly less muddled Christians assure us that 'the King's kids travel first class', the Bible—in typically earthy fashion—assures us that the religious man or woman who never has a pain never pays a price, and who never feels the Father's hand heavy on him isn't one of the King's kids at all but a bastard (Heb 12:4–8).

When Faith Hesitates

So, clearing the path of obstructions is useful. Seeing approximately where it leads is even better. But there is still the problem of doubt. Most of us suffer from doubt at one time or another. A painful crisis unresolved makes us wonder about all those promises of a prayer-answering God. Some detail or doctrine of the faith (as we understood it) does not stand the scrutiny of Scripture or experience. The Church can let us down bitterly; for a time its life and fellowship seem unreal, and the terrible thought steals into our consciousness that God might be unreal, too. More than one Christian minister has lost all sense of 'calling', and his very faith has been jeopardised.

What do we make of doubt? Is it an enemy of faith and of God? Am I sinful in even entertaining it? Is it wrong to ask God questions? If so, how is it that so many people in the Bible ask questions...prophets, priests and psalmists? What do I make of the fact that, in the experience of some people inside and outside of the Bible, the *struggle* to believe actually leads to growth, not decline? Is it even possible that honest doubt is an actual function of faith, not at all to be confused with sinful unbelief?

Another phenomenon, too, that is troubling many Christians and not a few leaders, pastors and preachers is this: We live in a time when faith is coming back onto the offensive after half a century (in Europe anyway) of defensiveness, apology and retreat. Theological liberalism with its rejection of supernaturalism and Bible authority is on the retreat. Evangelism, debate about Scripture inerrancy, healing ministries, reverent biblical scholarship, emphasis on signs and wonders, church-planting seminars...in many places there is advance and challenge and a new air of expectancy and optimism. Much of this is very good indeed—but the occasional note of warning sounds. 'Faith Formulae' prompted by extroverts with a stake in the mass-media promise instant health, constant prosperity and the answer to every prayer. 'Faith' is increasingly presented in terms of self-confidence, self-image and self-gratification. The old Bible words are being used, but with oddly different connotations. And the results vary. Some people bear ecstatic witness to what sounds like a universal panacea. Many others speak of disappointed hope and disillusioned expectation. Some are left dejected and guilty having been told that their faith is at fault or the Devil has scored a victory. Others are angry with men and with God...the Bible seems to have let them down. We are going to find that reservation and scepticism about some of these inflated half-truths, far from being 'unbelief' (as their advocates insist) is an expression of healthy biblical faith.

Faith will ask some hard questions. The outcome could well be stronger faith.

Note

[1] C S Lewis, *The Problem of Pain*, 1940 (Collins/Fountain: London, 1977 reprint), preface.

Chapter 2

Limits of Orthodoxy

Attitudes Before Answers

I used to preach a good deal in the open air. Only about 10% of the total population come indoors to church, so it seemed a good idea to go to the people rather than wait for the people to come to me. Market-places, factory gates and racecourses provided venues for telling out the Good News of Jesus. This introduced me to hecklers. One soon starts to recognise them. Rather pensive little men in raincoats who seem to have a great need to justify their own unbelief by pointing out the perceived faults in someone else's beliefs. So out came the old questions. Where did Cain get his wife from? Why did the Old Testament tell people to burn old ladies called witches? How could God make light on the first day of creation if there wasn't any sun until the fourth?

Christian courtesy seemed to require some stab at answering. Besides, they did me a favour by building up the crowd with their arguments; most casual passers-by enjoy a good verbal ding-dong. Some of those who stopped to mock remained to pray. But I soon noticed something rather pathetic about the regulars. *They never took any notice of the answers*. No matter how carefully I gave a reply, they trotted out the same questions next week. Their sole interest was in the questions. They didn't want answers. In fact they wanted their unbelief vindicated.

Now some people's questions about God in a world of pain are of this order. The very manner in which they are trotted out betrays the attitude. Like my atheistic friend in the previous chapter, they wield suffering as a weapon to draw blood in a verbal fencing match. 'Touché' is the only thing they want to say. Sometimes it is helpful to expose this fact.

I recall the university student who clearly thought no end of himself as he elbowed his way to the front of the crowd in Nottingham market-square.

'Do you believe in God?' he piped up.

I admitted this to be a fair summary of my state of mind.

'Have you ever *seen* God?' he pursued.

No, I freely owned never to have seen God.

'Then it seems to me that there is only one name for a man who believes in something he has never seen.' (He looked around for approval.) 'I'd say that was "a fool".' There was a thin scattering of applause.

He really was asking for it. Was I unkind? I asked him a question in return.

'Tell me, do you have any brains?'

'Why yes, I reckon so. I'm reading engineering at university. That takes some brains.'

I pursued it a little further. 'Have you ever *seen* your brains?'

He went rather pink. 'Well no, of course not, but...'

'No, of course not. Then what kind of a fool that makes you, I leave for the crowd to decide.'

There was a roar of approval from the audience. But it did more than score a point, for we moved into a useful discussion on the phrase 'seeing is believing' and eventually about Jesus' statement that without the new birth no one can 'see the Kingdom of God'.

The whole question of doubt, unbelief and faith has to be set against a wider question. What is my basic attitude to God? Why am I asking the questions? Do I want to believe, or do I welcome reasons to disbelieve? *Doubt*, I am going to suggest, can be a very good thing. I used to conduct a weekly 'surgery' for people who found faith difficult. I have the most precious and humbling memories of how often honest enquiry and even heartfelt argument could end with two people on their knees as one introduced the other to a living experience of God.

But *unbelief* is something quite different. It is part of the stubborn, sinful, fallen condition of humankind outside of God's grace and God's family. Both doubt and unbelief may point to the same problems and circumstances, but they function quite differently.

G K Chesterton recorded how a perfectly proper (if slightly sardonic) remark of his in a newspaper article was cut out as blasphemous. Someone called Grant Allen had written a book about the evolution of the idea of God. Chesterton wrote that it would be much more interesting if God wrote a book about the evolution of the idea of Grant Allen. Tongue in cheek, yes, but certainly not 'blasphemous'! That word should be reserved for a creature who airily dismisses his Creator as merely an 'idea'.

Chesterton makes a serious point. By the very nature of things, it is impossible for a mere mortal to put God on trial and ask a full explanation of the Creator's ways. As well expect the characters in a book to demand a full explanation from the writer. The author *is* the explanation; the characters only gain their existence from him. The self-assertion that puts *me* at the centre of God's universe and asks 'why doesn't everything suit *me*?' is a function of what the Bible calls *sin*...which may not show in immorality or thieving or blasphemy, but which puts self at the centre and God (if anywhere) at the circumference.

Thinkers in Search of an Answer

Three of England's most acute thinkers and writers this century wrestled with the question of seemingly irrational and meaningless suffering in a God-created world.

C S Lewis in fact outlined the most stunning arguments against belief in God by summing up the evidences of suffering, even of seeming malignity, in the world...and then went on to describe how a question one day occurred to him. Given these facts (and everyone knows them), how in the world have so many millions of people actually come to believe in God?

> The very strength and facility of the pessimist's case at once poses us a problem. If the universe is so bad...how on earth did human beings ever come to attribute it to the activity of a wise and good Creator? The universe...revealed by experience can never have been the ground of religion...it must have been acquired from a different source.[1]

G K Chesterton, in describing how he came to 'Christian orthodoxy' amidst the crashing of liberalism's bright hopes of human progress, told an amusing parable. He imagined an English yachtsman who thinks he has discovered a new South-Sea island complete with barbaric temple—only to realise that he has landed on the south coast of England and is in fact looking at Brighton Pavilion. The discovery is disturbing but delightful, for (as he put it to a friend at the time), 'what could be more delightful than to have all the terrors of going abroad combined with all the security of coming home again?'

What Chesterton is describing is his own pilgrimage. His insatiable curiosity forced him to explore all kinds of alternatives before at last he 'came home' to the instinctive belief of most human beings that 'God' makes more sense than 'No God', in spite of all the problems and unanswered questions! C S Lewis was to use a similar image when, in his first book after his conversion, he described a character's long journey round the world looking for the King who lives in the Castle on the Hill...who is in fact just behind his back when he sets out, and is waiting for him when he finishes his journey.[2]

D R Davies is my third example. Brought up in the squalor and injustice of a Welsh mining valley early this century, he turned his struggle against social evil into political protest and religious activism. As a Congregationalist minister,

> I believed the Kingdom of God to be something which Man himself could achieve. I started upon my ministry with a varied assortment of goods in my bag, but amongst them the one essential, fundamental thing was lacking—an experimental knowledge of God as Judge and Redeemer.[3]

Utterly disillusioned by the sufferings of the Depression and the failures of various policies and philosophies to grasp the depths of the problem, he travelled via humanism, psychology and Marxism to an eventual moral and mental collapse. In the process of actually trying to drown himself in the sea, he recalled some words of the Catechism as taught by his mother in his childhood:

I heard her saying—'Who is Jesus Christ?' to which I answered 'Jesus Christ is my Saviour' (the answer suggested by the catechism). It was just like that. A deep peace...flooded my entire being. I knew I had passed through the great tribulation. 'Rock of Ages—cleft for ME—naked come to thee for dress'. In the final anguish, hovering between life and death...I found God. And finding him, found everything.[4]

He struck out for the shore, survived, became a profound Christian apologist and writer, a minister in the Church of England. He was another who made a long journey only to discover that the final resting-place is the original point of departure—the reality of God as found in the life, death and resurrection of Jesus.

And the end of all our exploring
Will be to arrive where we started
And know the place for the first time.[5]

As with Lewis and Chesterton, the very presence of dark mysteries such as suffering and sin were the factors that *brought* him to God.

I experienced in my soul the bitter death of the illusions of the generation into which I was born, and lost myself in those illusions. But after that death I rose again, for I found myself in finding God.[6]

That is the paradox of faith. Put yourself at the centre and you lose everything, including yourself. Put God at the centre, and you find yourself. This is what Jesus meant by the danger of gaining the world at the expense of losing your own soul...and what Paul meant when he said, 'I no longer live, but Christ lives in me...I live by faith in the Son of God, who loved me and gave himself for me' (Gal 2:20).

Identifying the Real Problem

This is all splendid stuff. But it does not fully come to grips with the rather special kind of doubt that nowadays often troubles believer and unbeliever alike. For one thing 'orthodoxy' has not had a very good press lately. What Chesterton, Lewis and Davies meant by the word was simply mainline Christian belief as it has always been understood by most Christians. Lewis in fact referred to it as 'agreed, common, central or *mere* Christianity'.[7] Unfortunately, the phrase nowadays carries a flavour of cold correctness, dead credalism, stiff traditionalism and an unwillingness to listen, learn or bend. 'Bible Christians' can be like this. To say, 'I believe it because the Bible says so' is admirable and indeed essential. But it may become to some people (both those who say it and those who have it said to them) a mere entrenched dogmatism, devoid of sympathy, imagination or feeling. The 'counsellor' who only appears to listen to a troubled enquirer while he gathers breath and ammunition to fire, 'The Bible says...' is very little help. In fact he is not a counsellor at all. To say, 'I believe in the Bible' is one thing. To say, 'My personal interpretation of everything the Bible says is unchangeably correct' is quite another thing. But the two get muddled too often. The Bible is indeed uniquely, authoritatively and divinely true. But its truths cannot be shared adequately and convincingly just by shooting off cure-all texts.

'Orthodoxy' does little for the doubter whose

capacity to believe has been undermined by the subjectivism and secularism that fills the very air of our society and is breathed in every moment of life. Beginning university can be a devastating emotional experience for a Christian student from a 'good home'. One such girl told me of her first day. Entering the hall of residence, she was confronted by a publicity stall advocating lesbianism. Within 15 minutes her roommate wanted to discuss arrangements for one to disappear tactfully while the other went to bed with her boy-friend. The first lecture introduced a tutor whose entire mental and moral outlook was atheistic. Spirituality of any kind was clearly considered by the student body as probably meaningless and certainly irrelevant. The cumulative effect was numbing. That girl struggled valiantly for several terms, but eventually became another casualty.

In this kind of atmosphere (as prevalent on a factory floor as on a university campus) *truth* is simply not an issue. Arguments for 'orthodoxy' are simply irrelevant, since there is assumed to be no such thing as absolute truth anyway. If truth is a discarded commodity, what then is achieved by proving that something is true? The entire world of existence is open to question. All that one is left with is *experience*.

I once gave a talk to polytechnic students on 'Faith in God in a scientific age'. It was the kind of thing I had often done before. I was still recalling my own sixth-form days when science mattered more than any other field, and people suspected that modern knowledge somehow exploded biblical faith. On this occasion a sensitive young Christian did me the considerable courtesy of putting me right on a vital point.

'That was great stuff, Don,' he said to me,
'but it's not what the battle is now *about*.

You suggested that many facts support the claims of Christianity, and threw in the extra argument of the Christian's experience of God. But students nowadays are not interested in facts or logic. No one is sure any more that there is such a thing as fact, or such a thing as truth. *Experience* is all the rage. But the problem is, how can you tell one experience from another?'

As I listened, fascinated, he pointed out that various friends of his *experienced* transcendental meditation, psychedelic drugs, conversion to Buddhism, and the joy of becoming a convinced Marxist. He even told me of a friend who had 'experienced Jesus' at a mass evangelistic rally, and is very enthusiastic about it—but continues to be an atheist!

Afterwards, this young man and his splendid Christian friends gave me a copy, signed by all of them, of *The Gravedigger File* by Os Guinness, a kind of updated *Screwtape Letters* that deserves to be as widely read as C S Lewis's book. I sometimes look at those autographs with great affection. Out of the 14, 8 of them are young men I had personally led to Christ in previous years. They respected me enough to put me right where I had missed the boat in my understanding of what worries people today. I have several sections of the book underlined, including this one:

Secularisation is the acid rain of the spirit, the atmospheric cancer of the mind and imagination. Vented into the air not only by computer terminals, marketing techniques and management insights, it is washed down in the rain, shower by shower, the deadliest destroyer of religious life the world has ever seen...nothing is left to human spontaneity or divine intervention.[8]

Analysing Doubt

Doubt can be awful—a paralysing thing. It can muster a whole battery of different weapons, pounding at its victim in varied combinations so that he succumbs to what in 1914 was called shell-shock, in 1939 battle-fatigue, and in these enlightened days simply break-down. I was told by my English teacher years ago never to begin an essay with the words 'There are many different kinds of...' But I have to say it: There are many different kinds of doubt. The Bible is not uniform in the way it treats doubt, for doubt is not a uniform thing. At times it appears in Scripture as a close relation of sinful unbelief; at other times as the courageous questioning of faith; at yet other times as a sob of the sick or a cry of the helpless.

Job springs to mind immediately. Many a psalmist asks 'Why?' and 'Where is God?' Prophets such as Jeremiah and Habakkuk agonise over human anomalies and apparent divine injustices. In fact in the Old Testament—which makes up two-thirds of the Bible—one of the greatest themes is *quest* (questioning, querying, with only partly-answered questions). The New Testament has much more to say about faith and certainty, but is it not significant that the Old came first?

Yet faith is indeed the outstanding New Testament virtue. Jesus had some strong things to say about both unbelief and doubt. 'If you have faith and do not doubt...' (Matt 21:21). 'Why are you so afraid? Do you still have no faith?' (Mark 4:40). 'Stop doubting and believe' (John 20:27).

Os Guinness very helpfully analyses the five different doubt-related words used in the Bible. These carry connotations and implications such as *blown about* (James 1:6), *mentally split* (Mark 11:23), *hanging in mid-air* (Luke 12:29), *divided in opinion* (Luke 24:38) and *hesitating* (Matt 14:31).

> What follows from this is decisive...doubt is not the opposite of faith, nor is it the same as unbelief. Doubt is a state of mind in suspension *between* faith and unbelief, so that it is neither of them wholly and it is each only partly.[9]

I find this helpful and indeed convincing. From a more subjective viewpoint I would suggest nine kinds of doubt.

There is emotional doubt. The girl starting college suffered from this, as thousands do. An appalling feeling of helplessness, insecurity, even bereavement, afflicts the soul. 'Where is the blessedness I knew when first I saw the Lord?'[10] The feeling can be a *lack* of feeling too! A spiritual hypothermia numbs the soul, imperceptibly, inch by inch, until the doubter is so cold that he or she no longer *feels* cold and no longer wants to be warmed by faith. Someone recently told me that the last nine presidents of one college's Christian Union have eventually gone that way.

There is intellectual doubt. A sudden succession of arguments against trust in God (or confidence in the Bible) attack the mind. How on earth do I answer that? What on earth is the explanation for this? Yet it is almost inevitable that this kind of tension will arise. Very few of us have thought through every objection, examined every fact and grasped every implication before we came to Christian commitment. How could we?

There is disillusioned doubt. A friend of mine went through a very bad time in his career and his personal life—and found at that sensitive point that his minister not only failed to help him but turned bewilderingly against him. The consequent events have so hurt my friend that he has temporarily lost confidence in the Church...any church. As soon as he enters a service, however impressive it is to others, to him it all rings hollow. He thinks, 'My own church sounded as good as this, but in my moment of need it simply kicked me. Its fine words were a farce. So, in all probability, are these.' We can reply glibly that his faith in the first place should have been in God, not in God's people. But few of us have a purely God-centred faith. It is almost always God-plus-something that we believe in. That discovery itself may be ultimately strengthening, but the immediate experience can be shocking and crippling.

There is psychological doubt. I had spoken at a youth club on the fatherhood of God. A tough lad said derisively, 'My father yells at me and knocks me about—who wants another father.' Perhaps his particular response was at a superficial level. Deeper was that of a girl whose father molested her sexually. At profound levels of subconscious, the lovely word 'father' was to her a revolting title. She literally needed healing—and in her case received it, through counselling and prayer. How many are there like her, in some area of life deeper than the merely rational (and deeper than the level at which mere repetition of Bible phrases is enough)? If that shocks some Bible believers, let me pose a more familiar question. Why else is it that many good evangelicals who can give verbal assent and genuine heart response to God's grace and forgiveness are themselves legalistic and unforgiving? The experience of grace has somehow not reached the depths of the personality.

There is perspective doubt. Many of our problems spring from difficulty in seeing the whole picture. The once over-used word 'eternity' is now much underused. Yet eternity is the biblical perspective. Often a problem of the 'why?' variety is the more agonising because we are simply failing to see life as more than that brief spell between the cradle and the grave. The current Christian preoccupation with 'the Kingdom now' (good as far as it goes) runs up against some hard questions if it soft-pedals 'the Kingdom coming'. In biblical thinking, the Kingdom's future aspect is more than a negative 'not yet'; rather it is a heart-lifting 'not yet but assuredly coming', which enables the believer in the most trying situation to lift up his head and say, 'My redemption is nearer than it was.'

There is factual doubt. We simply come up against facts of which we were previously unaware. Years after starting Christian life in a pleasant church, someone discovers the horrifying facts about the Spanish Inquisition (Catholic), or Cromwell's massacre of Drogheda's citizens (Protestant), or the Salem Witches (Free Church). Someone comes to faith through the preaching of a man who later proves to be an adulterer or a thief (yes, it happens). He has his first experience of a Christian dying of leukemia. He discovers that although much recent archaeology does indeed confirm the Bible, the facts at Jericho seem to be in stark contradiction to it. It can be almost any kind of fact; the point is that we are previously unaware of it, and our present faith-system cannot take it on board.

There is situation doubt. I know a fine Christian man who came home one day to discover that something horrific beyond description had happened to his whole family. In some unimaginable way he pulled through. But many a Christian does not, in equally painful or much less painful situations. Something happens that seems to put a huge question mark over a fundamental assumption of Christian living, such as the love of God, or the reality of divine guidance, or the efficacy of prayer.

There is presupposition doubt. Many a supposed believer has made a happy start, only to come to grief a few months later in circumstances that then make one wonder what it was he imagined he believed. His presuppositions were seriously mistaken or inadequate. I recall a young girl who was the despair of her parents and left home to escape their reproach. Suddenly she became entranced by the companionship of a gang of young people from the local Pentecostal church. In no time at all she was not only speaking in tongues but sharply reproving her parents, and me her minister, for not being filled with the Spirit. A few months later she had found a different experience, and neither of the two churches saw her again. There had never been anything more than emotion and friendship to make her think she had faith in Christ. We all know similar examples. Crucial parts of the foundation are left out when 'faith' is built on mistaken or inadequate presuppositions.

There is doubt engendered by Satan. The Enemy will see to it that crippling doubts ensnare our path. It is vital to his interests that a Christian be robbed of certainty and sure-footedness.

A panacea, my dictionary tells me, is a 'universal remedy'. What is more admirable (and convenient) than one solution that always works? But the word has gradually come to have negative connotations. Panaceas, we suspect, claim too much. There is more than one problem, so one solution seems unlikely. Politicians are allowed panaceas, but only during election time. Real life is different. So it is with 'answers' to doubt.

Notes

[1]C S Lewis, *The Problem of Pain*, 1940 (Collins/Fountain: London, 1977 reprint), p 3.
[2]C S Lewis, *The Pilgrim's Regress*, 1933 (Collins/Fountain: London, 1977 reprint).
[3]D R Davies, *In Search of Myself* (Geoffrey Bles: 1961), p 68.
[4]*ibid* p 190.
[5]T S Eliot, 'Little Gidding', *Four Quartets* (Faber: London, 1959), p 59.
[6]Davies, *op cit*, p 214.
[7]C S Lewis, *Mere Christianity* (Collins/Fount: London, 1984 reprint), preface p 8.
[8]Os Guinness, *The Gravedigger File* (Hodder and Stoughton: London, 1983), p 61.
[9]Os Guinness, *Doubt* (Lion Publishing: Tring, 1976), p 19
[10]William Cowper (1731–1800). From the hymn 'O for a closer walk with God.'

Chapter 3

The Cross over a Suffering World

Paradox of Pain

It was rather like a scene from a second-rate thriller. I was definitely being followed. To make sure, I drove my car round three sides of a square, into an apparent cul-de-sac, and out of it through a narrow back lane. The car behind still doggedly followed. I parked behind the gas showroom (the purpose of my journey was to pay a bill) and my 'tail' slipped his car in neatly behind mine. The driver climbed out and followed me, while I uneasily tried to remember what I had said during a recent preaching trip in Ulster. As I came out of the shop he stopped me and asked, 'Excuse me, are you religious?'

It seemed that he had seen the Bible text in the back window of my car, and had followed me in the hope that I would stop. His problem? He was one of those immediately recognisable accident-prone people who for ever hover on the brink of disaster and sometimes wander over the lines drawn by the law. In a recent financial crisis he had more than wandered. He had, in fact, broken into a Catholic church and stolen the well filled poor-box. Now he was consumed with a semi-superstitious remorse. What could he do? I took him home, gave him a coffee, found him very ready to listen to a first-time explanation of the gospel, and led him in a prayer of commitment to Christ. We visited the priest together. He listened with stern sympathy, and promised to accept weekly repayments of the money. Finally, we stopped off at my friend's home and explained to a startled and rather sceptical wife that he had found God and begun a new life.

Two years later (now living 50 miles away) I had a desperate phone call from the same man. The little son of the family had been permanently crippled in a road accident. I caught the next train.

On the journey I prayed for wisdom in advising and comforting the family. Would their faith stand the test? The wife by this time had followed her husband into faith, but they were naïve folk, not readers, tending to lean heavily on experience rather than thought-out conviction.

Peter's first Epistle came repeatedly to my mind. Soon I was in their little street-house, sharing the first chapter (verses 6–9). We analysed the meaning of the rather complex sentences in a number of simple statements:

1   Gold is precious. Why? Because there isn't a lot of it.

2   Gold has to go through a refining process to purify it. If gold had feelings, it would certainly not enjoy the refiner's fire; but the result is the pure, genuine stuff.

3   Faith is even more precious than gold; it's even more rare. How many people in this street have any?

4   Sometimes Christians have to go through a stiff test. Peter calls it 'grief and trials'. God doesn't send the grief, but he can use it, like a refiner's fire, to make our faith stronger and more genuine.

5   We cannot see God; we cannot now see Jesus. But part of our faith is to be able to say, 'I love and trust the One I cannot see.'

6   Remember what faith leads to: something more

important than anything else—the salvation of your souls.'

They listened eagerly and drank it in. The wife exclaimed, 'Yes I can see that. Do you know, Mr Bridge, my husband really has been a new man since he met you. And now this. Two years ago, if this had happened, he'd have gone off and done something crazy—driven his lorry into a brick wall, or off a cliff or something.' Her husband nodded agreement. 'Pray with us, please. If faith has to get stronger the hard way, we must take it.'

My heart soared with gratitude as I left. Another cross-section of real life, with its pains and problems...yet making some kind of sense when faith takes its stand. The succeeding years have proved the reality of their faith.

Of course, we cannot explain every pain and peril as a test of faith. But this kind of thinking provides somewhere to begin. It is precisely to faith that the terrible questions address themselves. How can I believe, in the face of Downs Syndrome babies, earthquakes, starving African children, the torture of Russian dissidents, napalm, cancer, Beirut, Hiroshima...? The very assertions that faith insistently makes are most severely threatened by the paradox of pain. An ordered world created by God? The fatherly care of the Almighty? Love at the heart of God's being? It is this kind of perplexity that has led someone like Rabbi Kushner to suggest that God is not omnipotent. Dying David Watson pointed out:

> Kushner claims that God does not have the whole world in his hands, and therefore is not responsible for malformed children, for natural disasters, for fatal diseases. These simply live outside his jurisdiction.

However, if God is not in ultimate control, he cannot truly be God. If there is no final justice, no eventual triumph of good over evil, God is not the God who has revealed himself in the Bible and in the person of Jesus Christ... We cannot ultimately be sure of anything except being at the mercy of unleashed and unpredictable evil.[1]

World out of Joint

God made a perfect world, but planted in it something fraught with terrible risk: he made humankind with the built-in ability to choose. Free decision is part of being human—and an essential ingredient of love. We live in a world that both enjoys and suffers the consequences of thousands of decisions, good and bad—but especially bad. Sometimes the link between cause and effect, between bad choice and painful consequences is obvious on the surface. A disease is spread because people choose to have promiscuous sex. A town is destroyed because a tyrant chooses to unleash his army. Innocent civilians are maimed because a terrorist chooses violence rather than negotiation. Many (not all) die of lung cancer because they chose to go on smoking.

Sometimes the link is less obvious, but identifiable if you hunt for it. This planet produces enough food for all, yet millions starve. Look more closely and you find immoral economic policies, starvation used as a military weapon, corruption and bribery that syphons off charitable aid, superstition that leads to destructive customs...all decisions of a complicated corporate nature.

Sometimes the link seems non-existent. It is hard to

find any moral issue and any dimension of choice in an earthquake, a volcanic erruption, a flood, or a brain tumour! The Bible hints that the world is badly out of joint because it is a fallen world; that death itself is a consequence of sin, and an intrusion into the world God originally made. Precisely what that moral link can be with impersonal things such as landslides and tornadoes may not be clear, but we can think of analogies. Modern concern for pollution and environment, for example. Forests, seas, atmosphere, fish, climate; all are affected by human selfishness, pride and prejudice. Morality really can affect the deployment of immense natural forces and laws which at first sight seem completely unrelated to human decisions. Suddenly the apostle Paul's words appear as sober fact:

> The creation was subjected to frustration, not by its own choice...the whole creation has been groaning as in the pains of childbirth (yet it) will be liberated from its bondage to decay and brought into the glorious freedom of the children of God.
>
> (Rom 8:20–22)

Majestic ruin

A world made well, but fallen—that is what the Bible describes and explains. It is precisely what human observation and science describe, but cannot explain. It is also why, with equal force, atheists can point to disorder and chaos as apparent evidence that the universe is a meaningless accident—and the Bible can point to order and system as evidence of God the Creator.

What may be known about God is
plain...because God has made it plain. For
since the creation of the world God's invisible qualities—his eternal power and divine
nature—have been clearly seen...but their
thinking became futile and their foolish
hearts were darkened... Therefore God
gave them over in the sinful desires of their
hearts.

(Rom 1:19–24)

An illustration of this apparent built-in contradiction struck me as I stood beside the excavations of the
Pool of Bethesda in Jerusalem. Fifty feet down they
go, and at first sight they are pure chaos. Walls from
different periods cut across each other. Ashes and
rubble cover whole areas; the result of deliberate, sav-
age destruction. The wall of a Crusader fortress over-
laps the line of a Byzantine church. The ruins of a
mosque totter on the edge of a Jewish religious centre.
Chaos, and the grim reminders of warring cultures.
But look again—with the aid of a detailed archaeological plan—and behold, there is order. The five porticoes of the pool, mentioned by John the apostle, can
be traced. The church ruin follows the familiar line of
Byzantine architecture.

In fact, you can see the evidence of both sets of
facts. Here is *creative design*. Those porticoes and that
church could never have happened without architect
and builder. Equally, here is the *destructive intrusion*.
That ruin could not be so ruinous without the intervention of conflict and cruelty.

The Bible teaches that illness, death, hate
and ugliness are all signs and outward

manifestations of a state of ruin which over-
took a once-better world. It also teaches
that the signs of ruin are easily distin-
guished from the pools of order, love and
virtue which still bear testimony to the state
of the original edifice.[2]

The Decision that was Worth the Consequence

Follow this train of thought, and the question
changes. Instead of asking, 'Why did God make the
world so badly?' we now ask, 'Why did he allow it to
be ruined?' But that question has already been antici-
pated. He created a world open to risk because he
made it *open to choice*. Robots and puppets are incapable of love because they are incapable of initiative.
God's gift of free choice was both an expression of his
love and an invitation to our love.

Someone may well ask, 'Why offer it, when *wrong*
choice was not really a risk but a certainty?' We can
only assume that God considered the risk was worth
it. That should not be too hard to imagine since we
human beings often come to the same conclusion. A
man decides to marry the woman he loves. There is
the possibility that the one to whom he puts his heart
and happiness in hostage may betray him. There is the
certainty that one day death will intervene (till death
us do part). The happier the marriage, the more de-
vastatingly sad the parting. But thousands decide that
the risk and the uncertainty are worthwhile.

Freedom has other implications too. We are not
only free to hurt others; they are free to hurt us. There
is no exemption from the cost of living in a world of
free-wheeling individuals where choices bring them
into collision with each other.

'Why didn't God save my church-going grandma from being knocked over by a car?' asks some indignant unbeliever. But how, for argument's sake, would God stop her? By preventing her from crossing the road? By preventing the driver from drinking? Most people would welcome the first concept, but get very annoyed about the second. They would like God to prevent them from getting hurt, but would resist with indignation the idea that he might stop them womanising, drinking, gossiping or coveting. They would like an invisible wall of divine protection to keep out the hurt of other people (infecting me with their germs, mugging me, or stealing my job). But they certainly don't want the barrier to prevent them from hurting other people (with bad temper, sarcasm, lust or ambition).

The God Who Stepped In

All rather negative so far? The Bible goes on to tell us much more. God has not simply opted out of a world that resists his rule. That would effectively put us back in Rabbi Kushner's scenario. Instead, the Bible shows him constantly intervening in human affairs.

God warns

So many of the commands and threats of the Bible are God's love-warnings of the consequence of wrong choice. To see him as narrow, demanding and negative is to misunderstand totally his purpose and motive. After all, his purpose is to save us from hell, not to send us there! Imagine my neighbour about to set out with his wife and children in the family car. I notice that a tyre has worn thin and a blow-out is likely. I warn him about it. I don't expect him to turn on me in fury and accuse me of wanting to spoil the picnic, or of interfering in his private concerns. Least of all do I expect him to accuse me of wishing a blow-out on them. I warn them, not because I want them to have an accident, but because I don't want them to have one. God warns of discipline, suffering, judgement and hell not because he wants them for us but because he wants to save us from them.

God guides

The laws, rules, calendars and regulations which abound in some parts of the Old Testament are more than warnings. Modern Western society is at present learning the bitter lesson that 'permissiveness' is not freedom at all but a new form of bondage. We need walls around us: of order, pattern and instruction. Without them we are insecure, rootless and self-destructive. Within them there is a certain degree of security and shape. That is why the psalmist sings, 'O, how I love your law' (Ps 119:97).

God came

Dr Robert Oppenheimer, pioneer of nuclear fission, had to work hard to capture the interest of the authorities. He found that nothing served so well as personally calling, interviewing and lobbying. He commented, 'The best way to export an idea is to wrap it up in a person.' That is what God did. He did not just say something. He did not just send someone. He came himself. 'The Word became flesh and lived for a while among us' (John 1:14). We see in the Gospel narratives how that involved, not a Daniken-like visit from space, but true incarnation, with no dodging the cost of being human. *He shared our situation*. He knew poverty, hunger, thirst, temptation, tiredness, disappointment, indignation, injustice and pain.

During a time in hospital I chatted one day with the patient in the next bed. He told me he had a general kind of belief in God since 'someone, somewhere must have started it all,' but he couldn't see the point of Christians constantly going on about Jesus. That night I suffered pain and sleeplessness, and observed that he did too. I asked him next morning, 'Did you find last night that your belief in God helped you in your pain?' He looked surprised: 'No, how could it?'

'I don't suppose it could,' I replied. 'Not a vague God a million miles away. But my faith in Jesus helped me immensely last night, because I kept thinking, *'He knows what pain feels like.'*

This kind of reflection does not completely solve the problem of why pain is allowed. But the Christian is streets ahead of others in being able to meet that problem in the knowledge that God shares the pain.

> And when human hearts are breaking
> Under sorrow's iron rod,
> All the sorrow, all the aching,
> Wrings with pain the heart of God.[3]

God suffered and triumphed

But the Cross of Jesus is very much more than God sharing our situation. Christ's death was no mere martyrdom. In dying, he took on the combined forces of spirit-wickedness and defeated them. He embraced death on our behalf and broke its power. He evoked human badness into its worst-ever demonstration and exhausted its venom in himself. Most crucially of all, he united within himself the righteous anger of a holy God against sin, and the suffering that such sin deserves. This is the very heart of the gospel, one of those foundations for faith about which a come-for-help half-gospel does not speak clearly enough.

God will have the last word

One thing more must be said: the story is not yet finished. The Christian sees the whole human drama moving towards a goal which is in sight but not yet attained. It has many different names: the Kingdom, the Resurrection, the Eternal State, heaven, the Second Coming, the Father's House, the Day of the Lord. In any truly Christian approach to the present perplexities of life two facts about it are basic: it has not yet come; but it assuredly will come.

One of 1986's most popular television play-cycles was perceptively called *Paradise Postponed*. That postponement is due to the two factors hinted at in the series. First, human nature is very frail. Second, paradise depends for its fulfilment on something far beyond mere human effort and sociological tinkering. But the postponement is not indefinite. There is a terminal point in history which is in turn the doorway to eternity. Few people have put it more movingly and yet more simply than C S Lewis in the final paragraph of the Narnian chronicles.

> 'There was a real railway accident' said Aslan softly. 'Your father and mother and all of you are—as you used to call it in the Shadow-Lands—dead. The term is over: the holidays have begun. The dream is ended: this is the morning.'
>
> And as he spoke He no longer looked to them like a lion; but the things that began to happen after that were so great and beautiful that I cannot write them...it was for

them only the beginning of the real story. All their life in this world and all their adventures in Narnia had only been the cover and the title page: now at last they were beginning Chapter One of the Great Story, which no one on earth has read: which goes on for ever: in which every chapter is better than the one before.[4]

It has not yet come; it will surely come. Failure to grasp either one of these two facts will make inevitable a very bad crack in our faith foundations which will widen when the frost of creeping doubt gets into it. Today's emphasis on 'the Kingdom now' is healthy in many ways, and is overdue. Nevertheless, it must be held in balance with the more traditional emphasis on 'the Kingdom coming' otherwise the harvest will be disillusionment and lost faith.

Eternity provides the final riposte to that special category of dismayed faith that I have called perspective doubt. Is heaven a glorious reality? It should be. Longing for it can be nurtured within us by our communion with Christ whose presence will make it heaven.

Once, flying high over Kansas as the sun was rising, I actually saw the curve of the earth. For a few breathless moments I experienced a perception adjustment. The problems, pains and circumstances of this world were glimpsed from a new perspective. The Eternal Hope has that effect. It gives the lie to that numbing sense of unreality to which the twentieth century's arrogant and all-pervasive secularism can sometimes reduce us. Secularism is a gigantic confidence trick. Heaven exposes it.

Notes

[1] David Watson, *Fear No Evil* (Hodder and Stoughton: London, 1984), p 125. David was referring to Harold S Kushner, *When Bad Things Happen to Good People* (Pan Books).
[2] A E Wilder Smith, *The Paradox of Pain* (Harold Shaw Publishers: Wheaton, 1971), p 52.
[3] Timothy Rees (1874–1939). From the hymn 'God is love, let heaven adore him.'
[4] C S Lewis, *The Last Battle* (Collins/Fontana Lions: London, 1986 reprint), pp 171–72.

Chapter 4

Pilgrimage Without Pain

Faith triumphalism has performed a marvellous operation in recent years. Bible promises (out of context) have been so neatly sewn into the Western Dream of ever-increasing health, wealth, and happiness that you can hardly see the stitching. It takes rare skill to transform the biblical picture of Christian pilgrimage so that it has no Cross, no cost and no pain. But the promoters of the Faith Formula (including the prosperity cult) have managed it.

With magic phrases such as 'believe and receive', 'nothing is impossible', 'name it and claim it', and 'God wants you rich' these apostles of crossless Christianity have made it big. Some of them are mainline evangelicals, some are Charismatics and some are semi-heretical cult promoters. They are united in the new meaning that they have given to *faith*. It is not dependence upon God, but a *technique* for turning on the tap. These movements between them have gained the total commitment of thousands and a potential audience of millions, especially in America. Most of their disciples are starry-eyed extroverts already living in a prosperous consumer-oriented society. For every enthusiastic follower there must be four disillusioned wrecks abandoned by the wayside who now think faith is a fraud. Doubt, when addressed to these theories, is not a vice but a healthy and wholesome virtue.

Pathetic tragedy has sometimes followed, especially when the quest is *health*. The Faith Assembly sect based in Indiana, USA, provides an instructive example. Its several thousand members in six countries

number many genuine Christians who have 'gone all
the way' with the formula of claiming-and-confessing.
An estimated 80 people have died as a result—many
of them children deprived by their believing parents
of life-saving medical treatment. Several parents have
received prison sentences for withholding medical
aid. Attempts were made to indict the sect's leader, ex
Baptist minister Hobart Freeman, to no avail.[1] It is
not easy to establish in law that Freeman's advice and
teaching are directly responsible. Now he is past the
judgement of any human court since in 1985 he died
prematurely of untreated diabetes, a victim of his own
credulity.

Gnostic Mind-games

The basic brick of the Faith Formula is the assertion
that God has made promises to his children which he
is bound to keep. Faith involves not only believing
that the required blessing is offered but that you *have*
it. (The basis of this teaching is said to be Jesus' words
in Mark 11:24: 'Whatever you ask for in prayer, believe that you have received it, and it will be yours.')
A 'positive confession' is therefore required. You
must say openly and publicly that you have it, and
then you will get it. For this to work, faith must obviously be free from all negative thinking. Negative possibilities create doubt, and doubt destroys faith, so
God cannot act. Adherents are urged to 'practice
thought control (and) deliberately empty our minds of
everything negative concerning the problem, person
or situation'.[2]

'Positive confession' can take some curious forms.
A believer will 'show' his neighbours an empty plot of
land where he asserts his prayed-for new house is
standing. A lady I saw on television related how she

found a much-desired husband by 'positive confession'. She pictured his appearance, laid a place for him at the table, moved into a double bed and said goodnight before dowsing the light. Not surprisingly, she eventually found someone who fitted the bill and married him. The poor guy didn't have a chance. The sheer loopiness of all this is presented as an example of simple faith defying the wisdom of this world.

Enormous importance is attached to speaking the word of faith. Faith-healer Charles Hunter of Texas has no hesitation in claiming that the words of faith 'call into being something that does not exist at the present time'.[3]

Kenneth Hagin, an American evangelical, makes the same claim. 'Faith's confessions create reality,' he avers.[4]

Angels—we are told—surround us, eager to serve us and meet our needs. They won't start without our speaking to them the word of faith...and they can't move if you speak negative words. 'Your...words either put the angels to work or force them to step back, bow their heads and fold their arms.' This is the view of Kenneth Copeland, another major figure in the prosperity gospel.[5] However, negative thoughts can cancel out a spoken confession of faith. Kenneth Hagin writes:

> As long as you hold on to a confession of weakness, sickness and pain, you will still have these problems...Some man of God (praying) the prayer of faith for you...will be of no avail, because your unbelief will destroy the effects of his faith.[6]

This potentially heart-breaking cop-out explains how such teachers survive with equanimity the most abject failures of their own teaching...it is always the victim's fault. The effect on the devotee in terms of despair and self-condemnation can be easily imagined.

Charles Farah tells of a man lying in extremity on the floor of a church, the victim of a heart-attack. His frantic wife refused to allow the kiss of life or the calling of a doctor, for both would have been 'negative confessions'. Then, with mounting despair, she accused church members gathered around of not believing and expelled them from the chapel. Finally, the pastor had to go; his obvious concern suggested negative thoughts. The distraught wife watched her husband die, and after his body was taken to the morgue led a group of enthusiasts to gather round it to pray for a resurrection.[7]

Even more grotesque is the teaching that the apparent continuation of symptoms after the confession of faith is a demonic delusion. They have actually gone; the Devil is fooling you; hang on in faith and resist him. Some more extreme groups (not Hagin's and Copeland's) warn that to call a doctor at this stage would actually be fatal, as doctors are agents of Satan. Recourse to medical treatment now will not only cancel out the word of faith confession but will open the way to demon-possession. In his closing years, Hobart Freeman got as far as linking specific drugs and medicines with specific demons; the name of one was the name of the other. Anxious followers telephoned their aged parents for details of every childhood ailment and its remembered treatment so that the medicine-demons could be systematically named and called out.

Preliminary Objections to the Faith Formula

Most heresies are overstatements of one truth at the expense of another. Most harmful extremes spring from exclusive emphasis and exaggeration of otherwise helpful insights. This one is no exception. It can quote its impressive texts...out of context. But the whole trend stands condemned on a number of counts.

The Formula encourages selfishness and materialism

The underlying motivation is often simply to have *more*. At times it is promoted explicitly in those terms. A British magazine recently carried an article with some sound and biblical things to say about prayer and prosperity. Unfortunately, it carried a cover picture that epitomises the kind of TV commercial that portrays happiness through high spending. Two expensively dressed, well tanned people wearing carefully positioned jewellery and gold watches and carrying exclusive travel-cases smile happily in front of an airport departure-board of flights to exotic places, and finger their holiday brochures. Nothing wrong with any of it, but the 'image' spells the message clearly. Inside, amid some otherwise good teaching, there was an almost unbelievably crass statement drawn from the Gospel narrative of the soldiers gambling for Christ's seamless robe at the cross (John 19:23–24). Jesus, we are assured, wore some of the best clothes that money could buy. Of all the lessons that might be drawn from that poignant scene!

Raymond Kasch, an American pastor who has studied the prosperity phenomenon, comments:

Faith is desperately sought after in order to unlock the storehouses of heaven, so that the believer is showered with health and wealth and success. The consequence is a form of faith that is more interested in blessings than God's glory, a form of hope that is stimulated by a scripture-coated greed, and a form of joy that exists only as long as the heavenly spout is turned on.[8]

He commented wrily to me in Tallahassee, 'If a Faith Formula church were to be started in this town it would build up 500 members in a few weeks. Offered the choice of a Cadillac or a cross, guess what a lot of folk would settle for!'

Confronting such an approach, in irreconcilable contrast to it, is the inspired warning of Paul to Timothy:

Godliness with contentment is great gain. For we brought nothing into the world, and we can take nothing out of it... People who want to get rich fall into temptation and a trap and into many foolish and harmful desires that plunge men into ruin.

(I Tim 6:6–9)

The Formula promotes a false idea of God

The almighty sovereign Lord is presented as a celestial Santa Claus—a mechanical all-night bank into which you insert the required code (some formula of believing or claiming) and automatically receive what you ask. This is the essence of paganism: a deal in which I scratch a deity's back and he scratches mine.

The resultant caricature of man's relationship with God is without any moral content.

Recall, in contrast, the great confrontation at Carmel between Elijah and the priests of Baal (I Kings 18:22–38). The *baalim* in Canaanite worship were personifications of natural forces. The purpose of the cult was to keep these forces in action, to keep the seasonal cycle turning, to ensure that a man had sons, that his flocks multiplied, that his crops were harvested. An alliance between man and Baal was promoted to the advantage of both. Baal gave protection in danger, victory in war, fruitfulness in peace. To further this, the 'worship' provided energy to Baal by exciting it and stimulating its reproductive powers.

Challenged by Elijah, the priests of Baal worked themselves into a frenzy of such 'worship'. There was no moral content whatever. In contrast, Elijah represented 'the Lord who lives, before whom I stand' (I Kings 17:1), as King's ambassador, personally responsible, personally accountable, poised to listen and obey. Elijah symbolically represents moral issues: twelve stones to represent the unity of God's covenanted people, an altar symbolising their devotion, and prayer that presents the issue of loyalty to God.

In the Faith Formula there is little or nothing of this. The devotee would like a salary increase, a new car, instant relief from pain or poverty, and he engages in a technique devised to give him what he wants. Robert Schuller of America's 'Crystal Cathedral', for example, speaks of 'meditation in any form' (transcendental meditation, Zen Buddhism, yoga or prayer in the Judaeo-Christian tradition) as 'the harnessing by human means of God's divine laws'.[9] Notice who is sovereign in this Formula. Man 'harnesses' something impersonal—'divine laws'.

The Formula misrepresents the nature of faith

One Christian minister writes:

> Would it shock you to learn that God's healing power is available through your own mind and you can trigger it by faith. If you had *direct access* to your unconscious mind, you could command *any disease* to be healed in a flash. Jesus obviously had access to it, for he produced *command* healings.[10]

This is simply not what the Bible means by faith. It is a kind of pseudo-psychological mind manipulation in no way related to finding and doing God's will. Indeed, the writer has the impertinence to add that God has purposely placed this alleged power beyond our awareness because fallen human beings cannot be trusted not to tamper with it. 'However, there is a way to get to it—indirectly—*by faith*.' So faith is a technique for getting past God's ban!

This kind of twisted thinking is gaining so much credence in the West and elsewhere that genuine Christianity is in some danger of dispersing its energies in a flood of superstition, credulity and semi-magic, all of which are far removed from the faith of which the Bible speaks: surrender and assent to the will of God as revealed in his Word. The Christian does not say, 'I believe it because I want it and am determined to have it.' He says, 'I believe it because God says it, and I assent to his Word.' That is why 'Faith comes by hearing, and hearing by the word of God' (Rom 10:17 AV).

The Formula misunderstands the purpose of prayer

Norman Vincent Peale has given us his understanding of what prayer is all about. Much of his 'positive thinking' has found new expression in name-it-and-claim-it circles.

> Prayer power is a manifestation of energy. Just as there exist scientific *techniques* for the release of atomic energy, so there are scientific procedures for the release of spiritual energy through the mechanism of prayer...New techniques are being constantly discovered...*experiment with prayer power* (emphasis mine).[11]

Notice again the mechanical, impersonal and amoral nature of this view. Prayer is a technique that sparks off a mechanism for releasing energy. One might be talking about a computer using electricity, or a chemical mixture releasing gas. But, of course, prayer is an intensely personal communication with the divine and personal God. Where does the principle 'Your heavenly Father knows,' come into these techniques? What does positive thinking make of 'Abba, Father, everything is possible for you. Take this cup from me. Yet not what I will, but what you will' (Mark 14:36)?

The Formula makes nonsense of the Bible picture of discipleship

It is true, of course, that certain godly men and women prospered...eventually. It is true that God has made some very specific promises—some to the Jewish nation, some to the individual Christian (and it might be helpful to distinguish the two rather more often). But part of the call to trust God and follow Christ is a call to simple living, a call to hold loosely to this world's goods, a call to suffer unpopularity and loss for the sake of the cross-carrying Saviour. The cult of Christian prosperity is an insult to the imprisoned disciples in Russia, the poor disciples in South America, the hungry disciples of Africa. It is the abnegation of discipleship. It is the assertion that, contrary to Jesus' warning, you can put your hand to the plough and look back over your shoulder at the same time.

The Formula introduces a note of unintended cruelty

Triumphalism of any kind is always cruel. By its very nature, it can only work for a minority. There are simply not enough of this world's goods and resources to make every human being (or even every Christian) prosperous in the modern sense of the word. The average British citizen is almost inconceivably wealthy by world standards. His ownership of a motor car puts him in the top 5% of the world's population. The kind of prosperity promised by some advocates is simply a physical impossibility in anything but a small part of the world that establishes its standards at the expense of others. One such promoter of prosperity cheerfully admitted this to a friend of mine. When pressed to say whether, for example, Chilean Christians were lacking in faith and commitment, as witnessed by their poverty, he replied, 'That's a different culture from ours.' So 'biblical principles' taught in the Middle East 2,000 years ago are only applicable to North America and Europe in the 1980s! Meanwhile the Mexican peasant, the Masai tribesman, the Ethiopian refugee, the Russian prisoner, the unemployed West Indian in Liverpool, the victim of an Indian flood are, well, either lacking in faith, or the principle doesn't apply to them.

The whole scene of the Faith Formula, in its various manifestations, raises a number of very serious questions all bearing on the nature of biblical faith. One variation, for example, suggests that a kind of surrogate faith will do.

> You may not feel *you* have faith, but I will put your name on my faith-partner list, and I will pray for you every day. I will believe God to meet your every need and bless you with twice as much as you give. I will use *my* faith.[12]

Another version quite crudely links prosperity with the donation of money to a particular cause. For some, there is a more theological point involved: prosperity is promised by God and is the birthright of every believer. Some even say it is a consequence of the Cross.

For others again, prosperity is linked *in theory* with philanthropy. God wants us affluent so that we can share our plenty with others. 'True prosperity is the ability to use God's power to meet the needs of mankind' says Copeland.[13] Scriptures such as Ecclesiastes 11:1 and Galatians 6:7 are sensibly quoted. So is Paul's whole argument to the Corinthians about the cycle of giving-receiving-sharing-helping which so beautifully characterised the Early Church (II Cor 8–9). That is the theory. In actual fact the desire for more is often appealed to in the crudest of terms. 'I am what I have' takes a new twist with a religious flavour.

The use of the word 'prosperity' in Scripture is often referred to. But the references repay examination in their context. The promise to Joshua (1:8) is actually a military one; it concerns the conquest of Canaan by God's Israel at a unique point in the unfolding drama

of redemption. Nehemiah's promise (2:20) is again
very specific, and is to do with building Jerusalem's
broken walls amid the threats and sneers of hostile
neighbours. In a general principle it could certainly be
applied to work undertaken for God's cause, but it has
nothing to do with personal wealth. Psalm 1 (1:3) describes someone whose life is deeply rooted in God
and his Word: the 'prosperity' promised is clearly
linked to doing God's will. We shall see later how
Jesus himself handled promises from the psalter mis-
quoted by Satan to encourage presumption. The only
common New Testament reference (III John 2) says,
'Dear friend, I pray that you may enjoy good health
and that all may go well (AV that 'thou mayest
prosper') even as your soul is getting along well.' The
use made of this verse is tragic. We are asured that
God's will for your prosperity and perfect health is as
clear as God's will for your soul's salvation. In fact,
John's words are a standard greeting in letters from
that period, equivalent to a modern Christian finish-
ing a letter with, 'May God bless you in every way,
yours sincerely...' To read into this a promise of
wealth and health in the Atonement is absurd.

Claiming the covenant

Perhaps the most serious and impressive proof-text is
the combination of Genesis with Galatians:

> The Lord had said *to Abram*, 'Leave your
> country, your people and your father's
> household...I will make you into a great na-
> tion and I will *bless you*; I will make your
> name great, and you will be a blessing.
> (Gen 12:1–3)

(Christ) redeemed us in order that *the blessing given to Abraham* might come to the
Gentiles through Christ Jesus, so that by
faith we might receive the promise of the
Spirit.'   (Gal 3:14)

It is pointed out that Abraham became a very rich
man. Spiritual, physical and financial blessing were
given to him. All this, then, is guaranteed to us in the
gospel, for the gospel is the fulfilment of the covenant
with Abraham. 'If you make up your mind...to live in
divine prosperity and abundance, Satan cannot stop
the flow of God's financial blessing...You have exercised your faith in the covenant.'[14]

The first time I read that absurd *non sequitur* it
actually made me blush. I have read and studied and
believed the Bible so long, have gloried in its promises
and revelled in its logic and clarity, that it makes me
wriggle with embarrassment to see it so blatantly mistreated. Why do peple tear odd verses out of their
divine setting? God has given us a Word, not three
jigsaw puzzles jumbled together.

Put the mistreated verses back into context and
what do we get? The promise uniquely made to Abraham was to produce from him the people of God, and
through him the Messiah. This happened, and Paul
makes it clear that the fulfilment is for Gentiles, not
merely for Jews; for those, in fact, who share Abraham's faith in God. To *them* Christ came; for *them* he
brought about redemption, to *them* he gives his Spirit.
(See Galatians 3:6–14: the whole passage, not just the
last verse.) To ignore all this and to reason that the
'blessing' to Abraham (and therefore to us) is a lot of
camels and sheep is to turn into crass materialism
some of the most precious promises of the gospel.

The Faith Formula has, in fact, taken one of the

most basic evangelical covenant promises of the Bible and turned it into a slick formula for a good time in this world.

The Christian Experience of Father

Now, of course, there is a biblical doctrine of 'provision' (surely a better word than 'prosperity' with all the connotations that word now has). We are God's children. The fatherhood of God is not a vague, pious phrase but a glorious certainty that lies at the heart of the Christian gospel. In infinite grace and astonishing mercy, God has taken men and women who were rebels against his will and adopted them into his family. One consequence of this, in turn, is that prayer is *talking to Father*, including talking about needs of every kind.

> Ask and it will be given to you... Which of you, if his son asks for bread, will give him a stone?...How much more will your Father in heaven give good gifts to those who ask him!
>
> (Matt 7:7–11)

Confidence in God's fatherly relationship is presented by Jesus, in the most affecting terms, as the basis of *faith exercised for our human needs*.

> Do not worry about your life, what you will eat or drink...why do you worry about clothes?...The pagans run after all these things, and your heavenly Father knows that you need them.
>
> (Matt 6:25, 28, 32)

Indeed, Jesus had more to say about money, its use and misuse, its power and its perils, its needs and its provisions than about most other subjects. He never said that wealth is evil in itself, but he often warned of its dangerous and corrupting influence. It strangles spiritual growth (Matt 13:22). It diverts attention from real priorities (Matt 6:19–21, 25–33). It blinds us to genuine need (Luke 16:19–23). It threatens to master our life (Luke 16:13–15). It kills our concern for the soul (Luke 12:13–21). Its rewards are in the kingdoms of this world rather than the kingdom of God (Luke 6:20, 24).

How that is worked out in practice will partly depend on the age and the culture in which we live. Christians in Russia and China have outcommuned the Communists by living neither for the private individual nor for the state, but for the glory of God and the needs of others. I know one new Christian who has responded to the corruption and false values of the London Stock Exchange by becoming a scrupulously honest stockbroker, and another who has responded by giving it up and going into poorly paid Christian ministry. Some Christians responded in the Middle Ages with a vow of poverty; others in the seventeenth century with the Puritan ethic of hard work, frugality and stewardship; others in the eighteenth century with variations on Wesley's dictum, 'Make all you can; give all you can.' Modern equivalents are the return of some to 'tithes and offerings' and the commitment of others to community living.

Circle of generosity

What the New Testament teaches as a principle is the priority of the spiritual over the material, the commit-

ment of the Christian to a pilgrim life in loyalty to a
kingdom that is not of this world...and faith in our
providing Father. Part of that principle is the circula-
tion of money amongst Christians and churches,
through the sharing of those who have more with
those who have less. This is what Paul expounds in his
famous passage on church giving (II Cor 8—9). There
are beautiful principles here. Some of them are oddly
misapplied by the prosperity cult.

Supreme in Paul's mind is the example of Jesus:
'Though he was rich, yet for your sakes he became
poor, so that you through his poverty might become
rich' (8:9). (Unbelievably, this is actually quoted by
some as authority for the statement that there is prosperity in the Atonement. Jesus, we are told, died to
make us wealthy. Christ's death became our 'deed' to
all the elements of royalty—especially health and
wealth.)

Paul gives a picture of how generosity turns a rotat-
ing wheel of mutual help in the Church: 'At the present time your plenty will supply what they need, so
that in turn their plenty will supply what you need'
(8:14). To turn that into a guaranteed *quid pro quo*—
'Give to the Jerusalem poor and you'll find you get
twice as much back'—is an absurdity. And of course it
completely alters the motive.

Was Paul a believer?

However, neither Paul nor his readers had apparently
heard of the 'seed principle' so assiduously promoted
by some movements for the benefit of their own
funds. The Macedonian Christians gave generously
'out of the most severe trial...and extreme *poverty*'
(8:2). But where was their faith? Surely naming-and-
claiming should have got them out of their trial and

poverty. What were they doing wallowing in it with all those negative thoughts? Why were they poor, when God promised wealth to his people? And why did Paul not suggest that what they gave would be given back to them twofold? Even more mysterious—if the Jerusalem Christians were destitute, what was Paul doing sending money to them? He should have been asking for money from them so that they would get double back from God and therefore pay their bills. Possibly the explanation was that Paul knew nothing of the seed principle himself. It would seem not, for he has already described to these same readers how '...to this very hour we go hungry and thirsty, we are in rags, we are brutally treated, we are homeless' (I Cor 4:11). Why? He should have claimed in faith, or given half the amount he needed to receive, in order to deal with his hunger, thirst, rags and homelessness. Instead of learning to be 'content' with poverty or with plenty, with being abased and abounding (Phil 4:12 AV), he should have jacked in those negative thoughts and done a bit of 'positive possibility praying'. As for poor Peter, he seems to have known little about faith principles, because he had to admit, 'Silver or gold I do not have' (Acts 3:6).

We must stop teasing and address ourselves seriously to what the Bible does say about poverty, material needs, prayer and faith. There is a great deal.

Material needs are not to be despised. The Christian is not a spirit living reluctantly inside a body, trying hard to ignore it and think only of 'spiritual things'. As Archbishop Temple once said, Christianity is the most materialistic of religions. It tells us that we live in God's world, created and sustained by him. It tells us how God entered this world by incarnation, the Word made flesh. It shows Jesus battling against the sickness and pain that bedevils human existence. After death he rose physically, and took a body to heaven where he now feels our infirmities. He will return to complete the redemption of our bodies. Meanwhile the Holy Spirit indwells every believer, and our bodies are his temples.

Poverty and plenty can do equal damage to the soul. Jesus' warnings are addressed to the worldliness of the rich as well as the worldliness of the poor. To the rich he says, 'Do not store up treasures on earth' (Matt 6:19). Don't do it because it destroys your perspective (20), diverts your affection (21), distracts your attention (22–23) and divides your loyalty (24).

To the poor he says, 'Do not worry about your life' (6:25). To do so ignores the lessons of nature (25–30) and obstructs the exercise of faith (31–34).

Possessions are not evil in themselves, and can do great good. The 'communism' of the Early Church (Acts 2:44–47) was not a renunciation of wealth as incurably tainted; it was undertaken voluntarily and was not a 'condition of membership'. Peter tells the wretched Ananias that he had the right to do what he liked with his money; his sin was to lie about what he did with it (Acts 5:4). Paul's famous collection for the poor of Jerusalem would not have been possible if they had all shared the goods already. To the Corinthian church he teaches, rather, systematic and proportional giving (I Cor 16:1–2).

The New Testament warns against the restless itch to have more. Paul's words to Timothy do not promote legalistic asceticism, and need not make any Christian feel uncomfortable merely because (or if) he is prosperous. But the warning is solemn and clear (I Tim 6:6–11, 17–19). There are dangers in wealth, and a determination to get it will surely ruin the soul.

God does undertake to meet our basic needs and give us enough spare to give to others. The very possessions that may be a trap can also be a tool (II Cor 9:8). We should develop a giving lifestyle (Luke 6:38). Without slipping into a *quid pro quo* arrangement with almighty God, we can nevertheless rest on the assurance that 'giving' (of time, talent or tithe) will not be losing, but ultimate gain. Certainly we should not have the slightest hesitation about turning a financial need into prayer and childlike trust. Our Father is not too preoccupied to attend. Every Christian can surely bear witness to this from personal experience. We can trust our Father.

Right Words—Wrong Use

But we are still left with a problem. Is there not in fact a contradiction between the promises of 'the good life' in Scripture (so happily quoted by the prosperity prophets) and the warnings of a 'hard life' which freely sprinkle the pages of the New Testament in particular? I think we can suggest a few lines along which an answer can be found.

The Bible does not contradict itself. A balanced view of the Bible's promises and warnings must make room for both. The faith merchants over-emphasise one. Asceticism (making a virtue out of needlessly living hard) over-emphasises the other.

Without doubt, Jesus emphasises *cost* rather than *profit* in his picture of discipleship. That should be our joyful and willing starting-point.

Promises from the providing Father are to meet our *needs*, not our *greeds* (as my mother used to say during my childhood in the grim 1930s with my father unemployed and yet cheerfully giving to Christian work. Her definition of 'need' would be unacceptably low and spartan to many people now, but I was never conscious of deprivation or of parental anxiety.) God *will* supply our needs...he will also define what they are. I love the story of the missionary trainee who had enough cash to buy a one-way fare to a distant church, and was confident that the treasurer would give him enough to ride back. Nothing emerged, and a crest-fallen young man walked six miles back to college, complaining to God, 'I thought you would meet my need.' The whisper came to his heart in reply, 'I have. You needed to get your weight down.'

Promises should not be taken out of context. Deuteronomy is often enthusiastically 'claimed' not only by faith fanatics but by sober believers (eg 8:18; 29:9). But we need to be careful. These particular promises are addressed specifically to Israelites entering Canaan under a covenant with God that had clear conditions—the old covenant, not the new. No doubt we can learn a general principle from them: that obedience leads to blessing. But the primary and de-tailed application is not for us at all. We are not a theocratic nation living in a geographical promised land. We are a pilgrim people who belong to a King-dom that is 'not of this world'.

That brings me to my final suggestion. God is al-ways concerned about our ultimate spiritual good *above* our immediate physical good. That is not to say that the body does not matter. It does. But the spirit matters more. This is why Jesus tells us to make our first aim God's kingdom, God's reign, God's will, God's righteousness...and promises that if we do, the lesser will be included within the greater. 'All these things will be given to you as well' (Matt 6:33). Where is our treasure? What do we set our hearts upon? 'Store up for yourself treasures in heaven... For where your treasure is, there your heart will be also' (Matt 6:20–21). Faith finds that to be so because faith has al-ready said, in defiance of a society obsessed with things, that the King matters more than the thing.

Notes

[1]Report in *Christianity Today* (November 23, 1984).
[2]*ibid*.
[3]Charles and Frances Hunter, *To Heal the Sick* (Hunter Books: USA, 1983), p 64.
[4]Kenneth Hagin, *How to Turn Your Faith Loose* (Faith Publications: Tulsa, 1983), p 23.
[5]Kenneth Copeland, *God's Will is Prosperity* (Copeland Publications: Fort Worth, 1982), p 91.
[6]Hagin, *op cit*, p 29.
[7]Charles Farah, *From the Pinnacle of the Temple* (Logos International: Plainfield, 1985), chap 7.
[8]Raymond F. Kasch, *Confronting the Faith Formula Error* (Privately published. Available from PO Box 12937, Tallahassee, Florida, USA).
[9]Robert Schuler, *Peace of Mind through Possibility Thinking* (Fleming H Revell: USA, 1977), pp 131–32.
[10]C S Lovett, 'The Medicine of Your Mind', *Newsletter* (August 1979).
[11]Norman Vincent Peale, *The Power of Positive Thinking* (Fawcett Crest: USA, 1983), pp 52–53.
[12]Kenneth Copeland, *The Laws of Prosperity* (Copeland Publications: Fort Worth, 1982), p 26.
[13]Kenneth Copeland, *God's Will is Prosperity*, p 37.
[14]Donald B Kraybill, *The Upside-Down Kingdom* (Marshalls: Basingstoke, 1978), p 113.

Chapter 5

Sickness, Healing and the Human Mind

We watched in silence as the young lad was carried into the ambulance. His rare blood disease had come to a critical stage. Life was certainly in danger. His family (members of the church) had already suffered several bitter blows but were clinging to their faith in God.

My heart ached as I watched. I longed to give him the laying-on of hands there and then. What held me back was a perennial problem: *what if it didn't work?* Would hope raised and then crushed only add to the already intolerable burden? I silently prayed instead. Next Sunday while conducting the church inter-cessions my voice broke and I quietly wept as we prayed for him.

Two weeks later, the astonishing happened: heal-ing. The doctors carefully explained that they could not pronounce him technically cured until a year had passed without recurrence. The 12 months elapsed, and the lad's mother saw the final words written across his case-sheet: *inexplicable healing*. He is an adult now.

But more blows were to follow. A few years later his brother was plunged into the horrors of a brain tumour. Clergy, schoolteachers, church members, schoolchildren and neighbours gathered for a day of prayer. Major surgery followed...long months of treatment...then, painfully slowly, recovery. The boy discovered that certain glands had been destroyed and he would never grow any further physically. Some-where along the weary way a very special faith developed. He sensed a call of God to serve afflicted children. His deeply moving account of his own sufferings won an award from the national newspaper which published it.

That story epitomises so many of the mysteries of sickness and healing as it relates to Christian faith and the message of the Cross. The whole issue is currently a storm-centre of great controversy in Christian circles. Here is a very emotive subject. Picking your way through the various opinions, theologies and experiences available is like pursuing a walk through a Cornish moor without a map in a fog. Some slips and a lot of mire are virtually guaranteed. As I write, a Christian doctor of great faith and experience has just telephoned me. He has no doubt of the reality of the supernatural. Yet he says, 'Pick out 100 lepers who have come to my mission hospital for treatment. You pray for 50 of them, and I'll give the other 50 the best available medical treatment. We both know which 50 will get better—mine!'

It is an interesting point. Of course, the efficacy of prayer can never be proved by statistics; God is not a prescription service at our disposal. Nor is there any contradiction between saying our prayers and taking our medicine. What my friend was reacting against was the kind of thing so often introduced by free-wheeling itinerant faith-healers who sweep into town heralded by melodramatic publicity, snipe at doctors with references to the sick woman in Scripture who spent all her money on them but only got worse, offer guaranteed healing to all who truly believe, and then sweep out again. Left behind are a few successes, disappointed or self-condemning believers to whom nothing happened, and the local doctors patiently ministering to hundreds whom the visiting preacher never met.

Yet God does heal at times. Only a week before my friend's telephone call, another Christian doctor was interviewed by the BBC. He had just published a book in which he relates and analyses indisputable cases of physical healing in answer to prayer. (I know some of them personally.) His research brings him to three conclusions: physical healing happens; there is no automatic correlation between faith, sound theology and the experience of healing; only a small proportion of those seeking divine healing actually obtain it, but the number and the proportion is rising as churches become more committed to a healing ministry. In those three conclusions are encapsulated most of the painful puzzles that abound in this subject.

I don't want to be thought of as a disbeliever in divine healing. I believe in it...when God chooses to grant it. My belief is not pure theory. I have witnessed several healings in response to various approaches of ministry—anointing with oil, laying-on of hands, administering of Communion, silent prayer, the dismissal of demons, even direct healing as I was preaching and the sick person listened. *But faith is not something that flies in the face of facts.* So when we consider the issues of doubt and faith we must hold on to both: our awareness of factual reality and our faith. The Faith Formula teaching we considered in the previous chapters ignores facts and thus makes faith into foolishness.

Shamanism and Magic

An extrovert with a magnetic personality can easily slip into the traditional role of the witch-doctor of animistic societies. The word 'shaman' is an anthropological term used to cover men and women found in most cultures and periods who claim direct access to the 'spiritual world'. Certain techniques of meditation, trances, visualisation, drugs, breath-control, auto-suggestion, hypnosis...all of these are shaman stock-in-trade. It is worrying to see them reappearing with increasing frequency among Christians.

For example, Morton Kelsey, an Episcopalian priest whose scholarship and insight has helped many, writes:

> Jesus was a man of power. He was greater than all the shamans...my students begin to see the role Jesus was fulfilling when they read Mircea Eleade's *Shamanism*... This is the same kind of psi power Jesus himself had... Those who are taken aback by His healing ministry are ignorant of the experiences of healing universally known...in most forces of Shamanism.[1]

Agnes Sanford was a pioneer thinker and writer with many biblical insights, and is increasingly quoted by Christians involved in healing. Yet some of her ideas seem open to question. What, for example, is one to make of the suggestion that 'Spirits of those (dead) for whom we have prayed on earth are working through us.'[2]

Equally difficult to distinguish from age-old methods employed by pagan mystics are the visualising techniques sometimes called 'imaging' or 'imagineering'. By these methods, it is claimed, the Christian's thoughts actually create reality and bring desired objects into being.

The Bible speaks in the most specific terms against any dabbling with 'detestable ways...divination, sorcery, witchcraft...one who is a medium or spiritist or who consults the dead' (Deut 18:9–13). The reason given here (and by Isaiah) is interesting. God is promising a long line of prophets and inspired writers; their work would culminate in the coming of the Son of God. To consult the shadowy world beyond the curtain is in effect to say that God's testimony in the Bible and Christ is not enough. 'When men tell you to consult mediums and spiritists, who whisper and mutter, should not a people enquire of their God?...To the law and to the testimony' (Isa 8:19–22).

The Bible gives frequent warnings of the danger of false prophets who may deceive even God's elect (Matt 24:24; I John 4:1–3). Our own generation has seen examples of fundamentalist leaders ensnared in their own power over people, and pushed by their own promises into ever more dubious techniques for getting the promised result. Jim Jones of the Guyana massacre was once an acclaimed evangelist. Moses, the leader of the Children of God cult, was once invited to the Filey Bible Convention!

Sickness and Healing in the Bible

Healthy scepticism, then, may well be a necessary function of faith when meeting the claims of some faith-healers. Nevertheless, a balanced and sober healing ministry is being conducted in many areas of today's Church. How can the two be reconciled? Is a healing ministry truly biblical? On some issues most Christians agree: sickness is one of the consequences of sin; not every sickness is directly related to specific sin; Jesus confronted sickness and healed many, as a sign of the kingdom of God; and faith is one vital fact in the healing ministry.

But where does this lead us (or leave us)? Is it true that sickness was in some way dealt with at the Cross?

Is sickness never God's will? Has the Church a mandate to heal? Most acutely—does faith invariably bring healing? Anyone with any experience must say 'No' to that last question. And yet...and yet...there are those oft quoted scriptures...They are beautiful and moving words:

> But he was pierced for our transgressions,
> he was crushed for our iniquities;
> the punishment that brought us peace was
> upon him,
> and by his wounds we are healed.
>
> (Isa 53:5)

This was clear reference to the work of Christ upon the Cross. The whole context (the pinnacle of Old Testament messianic prophecy) makes that clear. The verse that follows is one of the Bible's clearest expressions of 'substitution'.

> We all, like sheep, have gone astray,
> each of us has turned to his own way;
> and the Lord has laid on him the iniquity of
> us all.

Evangelicals love the words and what they imply in terms of forgiveness of sins freely given to us at awful cost to God. Yet Pentecostals rightly point out Matthew's use of this prophecy:

> Many who were demon-possessed were brought to him, and he drove out the spirits with a word and healed all the sick. This was to fulfil what was spoken through the prophet Isaiah: 'he took up our infirmities and carried our diseases.'   (Matt 8:16–17)

From this the conclusion is drawn. Christ bore our sins upon the Cross. Those who come to him in faith will instantly find forgiveness. There is no 'perhaps' about it, no 'if it be his will'. All agree on that. But Christ also bore our sicknesses. So those who come to him in faith will instantly find healing. No 'perhaps', no 'if it be his will'. He has *declared* his will.

Finally, Peter is quoted to complete the case.

> He himself bore our sins in his body on the tree, so that we might die to sins and live for righteousness; by his wounds you have been healed.
>
> (I Peter 2:24)

Sin-bearing and healing took place at the Cross for those who, 'were like sheep going astray, but now...have returned to the Shepherd...of your souls' (I Peter 2:25).

Here is the rub. These very words are often used to bolster the teaching that brings self-accusation and disillusionment to many who believe and yet are not healed.

More than one meaning

The achievement of Christ's Cross is too vast to express in any one formula of words. But at its very centre is God's response to sin. The greatest human problem is sin, which estranges us from God. Until that gulf is bridged, all else pales into insignificance—like offering aspirin to a man in a condemned cell. That is the problem Isaiah and Peter address. The context is clear. 'Healing' is a metaphor for salvation from sin, obtained for us by the sin-bearing Saviour.

Matthew says something quite different. His subject is Christ's healing ministry. He tells us what Jesus achieved in his life, not his death. Not what he bore for us in his passion, but how he bears *with* us in his compassion. That is Matthew's topic.

Then in what sense did Jesus carry our sickness? Clearly, not in the sense that he carried our sin. For sin he bore the Cross, paid the penalty, offered the sacrifice, engaged in the glorious exchange whereby he (the sinless) carried our sin, and we (the sinful) are counted as sinless (Gal 3:13; I Peter 2:24; Heb 10:12; II Cor 5:21). The same words simply cannot be used in the same way for sickness; he was not made sickness for us; it is a meaningless concept. He did not offer himself a sacrifice for sickness. Of course, there is a connection between his death and his healing ministry, for his death (and resurrection) is that which authorised, enabled and equipped him to be everything that the believer finds him to be: Saviour, Redeemer, King, Healer, Lord. But there is no direct, infallible, guaranteed cause-and-effect equation that covers sickness as it covers sin. The believer *is* saved by faith; not sometimes but variably. The believer *may* be healed by faith; not invariably, but sometimes. Someone as committed to divine healing as John Wimber nevertheless rejects the idea of healing in the Atonement. He argues that healing is one result *of* the Atonement, is available at God's sovereign discretion *through* the Atonement, but is not guaranteed *in* the Atonement.[3]

Some other biblical descriptions of Christ's achievements provide helpful analogies. It soon becomes obvious that not every benefit of the Atonement is immediately available. Christ 'tasted death for everyone' (Heb 2:9). But believers still die. What they are instantly delivered from is the judgement that otherwise follows death. In dying, he destroyed 'him who holds the power of death—that is, the devil' (Heb 2:14–15). But the Devil does not cease to exist. It is *fear of death* (one of his favourite weapons) that is destroyed. Jesus 'triumphed' over the principalities and powers at the Cross (Col 2:15). But they do not stop attacking us. Faith stands against them, but the conflict only ends when earthly life ceases. Jesus shared and experienced our humanity and our temptations (Heb 4:14–16). That does not mean that faith banishes temptation and obliterates our human infirmity. Jesus announced the kingdom of God (Matt 4:17). That does not mean that every feature of the Kingdom is now fulfilled, and that every knee yet bows to him.

So with sickness. It can never be quite the same again, since Christ came, lived, died, rose and sent his Spirit. Like death itself, it has 'lost its sting'. But it has not gone away.

When Sickness Strikes

How viciously it strikes! 'Sickness', in fact, is a rather innocuous word, suggestive of a time in bed, lovingly cared for, catching up with our reading. The reality can be far worse: Disease. Pain. Distress. Weakness. Fear. Panic. Waiting for the X-ray results. Trying to read the truth in the doctor's eyes. Tears. Sleeplessness. Helplessness. Embarrassment. Unemployment. Dwindling savings. Does God care? Why did he allow it? What do I pray for?

How much faith-corroding doubt is attributed to illness, I do not know. Long observation as a pastor makes me think that few Christians actually lose their faith solely because of disease and imminent death. Those who watch, I suspect, are more prey to the agonising questions. My personal experience is limited. For 14 years, in childhood and youth, I knew almost constant asthma, with the fear, moroseness and insecurity that often accompany it. Night-time was something to dread. Yet two-thirds of the way through that period, God converted me, and I never recall finding it hard to reconcile his love with my asthma. But then, before conversion, my mind was already immersed in Scripture from my Brethren background. The wisdom of God's will, the passing nature of this life and its allurements, the glorious reality of heaven, the supreme bliss of simply knowing Christ—these were all counterweights.

Within 10 years of losing my asthma, I had an accident in the course of evangelistic work which left a permanent back injury. Hospitalisation, recurring pain, constant inconvenience, the inability to sit in a relaxed position, occasional periods of more severe pain, when lying on a hard floor was the only way to get partial relief...that was the story for the next 30 years. Now there is a partial but very remarkable healing through the laying-on of hands which has brought blessed relief from pain.

During that time I have pondered on the subject a great deal. I have seen some people remarkably healed under my own ministry—organic healing, acknowledged by doctors. I have 'believed' for healing myself...and have willingly availed myself of skilled medical treatment, both 'orthodox' and 'alternative'. Why have I been ill? There are few mysteries and the answers are obvious.

My particular case of asthma was the product of a difficult birth, childhood poverty (resulting from social injustice) and medical ignorance—in other words, a world out of joint. I live in such a world. It is not how God made it, and one day it will be different.

Meanwhile, the asthmatic condition made me extremely sensitive to people who are nervous, frightened, depressed, suicidal, insecure. Better training for the Christian ministry than any training course!

What would I do if really bad illness were to come? I don't know, and I feel uneasy when the thought occurs to me. I have to fall back on observation. Some of the people I have introduced to Christ have died of the most appalling illnesses. Serenity has marked their progress. Grace is obviously given in the measure of one's need for it. Lessons in faith and patience are learned; character is trained.

Advice for the Sick

With the onset of the first symptoms I do three things, in this order: I pray, telephone the doctor, and seek prayer and ministry from mature Christian friends in accordance with James 5:13–16. Soon the question, 'Why this time?' pops up. I consider the biblical possibilities. Fatherly discipline? Perhaps. If the reason is obvious, I try to deal with it. If I can think of no obvious reason, I don't get hung up on it. There are other possibilities. Is my faith to be strengthened through stress? Quite possibly: faith is more precious than gold. Am I simply suffering because I still live in a groaning world, and together we await that future deliverance in which God's children will take such a leading part? Is there some deeper discovery of the grace and help of God, which can only be made in pain? Is God using this apparent set-back to move me into a different sphere of service? Have I a testimony to share with someone who will not be impressed by anything less than a view of triumphant fortitude? Or is this one of those examples of suffering which simply cannot be explained in this dimension of space and time because it has causes and consequences in another dimension?

Quite certainly there are things which God will want to say to me. He reminds me that I am a pilgrim, and 'this world is not my home'. He wants to make heaven more real to me. The very failure of comfort and the temporary disappearance of euphoria and a sense of well-being remind me that when all comes to all, my total dependence is not on the way I feel, but on the Saviour I know. 'I dare not trust the sweetest frame, but wholly lean on Jesus' name.'[14]

David Watson, in his last book, completed shortly before he died, and with the tentacles of terminal cancer beginning to tighten their hold, recorded in writing his exercise of thinking aloud about sickness. Where does the kingdom of God come into this? Is suffering sometimes punishment? May suffering sometimes be a test? What is God saying to me? He reread Job. He pondered on some of the insights of C S Lewis. He welcomed the prayers and ministry of John Wimber. He recalled again the story of Joni Eareckson, paralysed since her teens yet bringing confidence and faith to many. He talked to an African Christian torn and ravished by terrorism, who passed on the comment, 'God never promises us an easy time; just a safe arrival.'[5] He found a few partial answers—and many, many tokens of God's goodness and grace. His final words expressed an attitude rather than an answer. 'Father, not my will but yours be done. In that position of security I have experienced once again his perfect love, a love that casts out all fear.'[6]

God's will—that is the ultimate resting-place. His will may well include healing...this time! Welcome prayer from others with a proven ministry—especially within your own church community. Meditate often on the marvels of self-healing and built-in immunity which God has created within you. Avoid, as far as possible, worry, fear, self-pity, bitterness and panic. Pray often but briefly; sickness is not a time for prayer marathons but rather for resting in God's character.

If—this time—healing comes, by whatever route, slowly or quickly, through prayer or medicine, I see it as from God. Yet always there is a note of caution. I must die one day. Christ's redemptive work is complete as far as my soul's salvation is concerned, but is still being worked out in my character, and is still largely future in my body. The time has not yet come when, 'the perishable must clothe itself with the imperishable...and the mortal with immortality' (I Cor 15:53).

Until then, there are mysteries. The very necessity of faith, so often underlined in the New Testament, implies a certain degree of darkness, ignorance and perplexity. It is precisely in the context of a groaning world and a not-yet-complete redemption that Paul warns,

> If we see what we hope for, then it is not really hope. For who hopes for something he sees? But if we hope for what we do not see, we wait for it with patience.
>
> (Rom 8:24–25 GNB)

In that word 'hope' rests the best answer to the most painful perplexity of illness, namely its frequent pointlessness. What do I make of my sickness (or that of my friend) when there seems no cause for fatherly discipline, when rather than create patience it promotes despair, and when faith is not so much called forth as mocked by the weariness of an indefinitely delayed answer? Yet can something really be pointless when it is an ingredient in that process through which (says Romans 8:18–25) a groaning universe is moving towards its share in the coming glorious liberty of the children of God?

Notes

[1]Morton Kelsey, *The Christian and the Supernatural* (Augsburg: USA, 1976), p 93; *Healing and Christianity* (Harper and Row: New York, 1976), p 51.
[2]Agnes Sanford, *The Healing Light* (Macalester, 1947), p 113.
[3]John Wimber with Kevin Springer, *Power Healing* (Hodder and Stoughton: London, 1986), chap 8.
[4]Edward Mote (1797–1874). From the hymn 'My hope is built on nothing less'.
[5]David Watson, *Fear No Evil* (Hodder and Stoughton: London, 1984), p 141.
[6]*ibid* p 171.

Chapter 6

Faith, Doubt and Presumption

The best time to examine the sun is during an eclipse. Outlined against the moon's dark shadow, we can get some idea of the glorious corona as it really is. A good look at the blemishes and confusions of triumphalist credulity will help to show, in the same way, what faith really is. Healthy scepticism in this realm helps us to see what faith is *not*, and moves us toward some understanding of what it *is*.

Faith Is Not a Technique for Tapping Power

The very use of words such as 'technique' and 'formula' lets the cat out of the bag. But God does not invite us to believe in faith; he invites us to believe in him. Not the size of our faith but the size of our God is what counts—as Jesus' reference to the mustard seed implies (Matt 17:20).

Faith Is Not a Rival to God's Will

A mark of Christian maturity has always been submission to God's will. Like Joseph in Egypt, believers have learned to say in the most adverse of circumstances, 'God intended it for good' (Gen 50:20). The words 'thy will be done' stand at the heart of the Lord's Prayer. The picture of Jesus kneeling in Gethsemane, surrendered not to his own will but the Father's, is prayer at its highest peak. It is precisely here that Faith Formula becomes a caricature of faith in action. God does not spring to do my will; I bow to do his. In days of enthusiasm and renewal, it is dangerously easy to force God's will into our vision. It won't do.

Faith Is Not to be Confused with Presumption

A site in modern Israel haunts my imagination. The south-eastern corner of the temple mount is now reliably identified with the 'pinnacle of the temple'. A fallen stone has been disinterred with the inscription 'The Place of the Trumpets', confirming that this was the focus of attention for the whole populace as the silver trumpets blasted out the call to assembly and festival. The place reminds me, of course, of that deep and searching story of Christ's temptation (Matt 4:1–11).

The story, which could only have been passed on to the disciples by Jesus himself, is full of the most profound truths. Here is the Master, fresh from that awesome moment of baptism (when the Father declares and the Spirit seals his unique Sonship), now plunged into the most searching and perilous exploration of what it means and what it may lead to. 'If you are the Son of God'…then turn stones into bread, perform a miracle of self-deliverance from the temple roof, and bring the world to your feet by your personality and power. Some of my friends may wonder wherein the *temptation* lay. What was wrong with any of that? But the first suggested act was an inducement to *presume on his Sonship*, to provide food the easy way and avoid the cost of incarnation. No Saviour here for the Ethiopian refugee and the hungry Asian peasant. As soon as becoming man begins to hurt, hide behind your deity. But he refused that path.

The second temptation took the 'reasoning' further. It was the invitation to *prove his Sonship* by forcing the Father's hand. 'I've got into this place of public danger—you've got to get me out of it for your own reputation.' Jesus hears in this not the formula of faith, but the hiss of Satan.

The third came right out into the open. It is the invitation to *abandon Sonship* in an act of people manipulation familiar to every political and religious mass-leader whose exploits filled the pages of history yesterday or still dominate the pages of newspapers today. No doubt it would have worked for a while. But the Father had another way. 'Ask of me, and I will make the nations your inheritance' (Ps 2:8). Again the false path is rejected.

Devil's view from the temple roof

The attentive reader will have noticed already how relevant these temptations are to the Christian who knows something of renewal and is really getting somewhere in his sense of sonship and anointing. The second temptation in particular is discomfortingly pertinent to the whole issue of holding back in 'doubt' and acting in 'faith'. But when does a leap of faith become presumption? And when is hesitation the warning voice of conscience, conviction and the will of God?

'Throw yourself down. For it is written...' And the Devil quotes the Bible itself. Act in the abandonment of faith. Pin everythig to a faith-promise. 'The terrible thing about the tempter's question is that it is such a pious one,' says the perceptive German preacher, Helmut Thielicke. It quotes the Bible and 'takes God at his word'.[1]

But we can only truly take God at his Word by placing ourselves under it. Satan's invitation, so apparently splendid in its positive faith affirmation, was an invitation to come out from under the will and Word of God. 'Force the pace on God' was what it added up to. But the whole context of the psalm from which the Devil so piously quoted is one that excludes the action he proposed. 'He who dwells in the shelter of the Most High will rest in the shadow of the Almighty…if you make the Most High your dwelling' (Ps 91:1, 9). Here is a picture of someone who walks God's way, and acknowledges God's sovereignty. What Satan proposed was to force God's hand.

Research into the popular messianic expectation of that time casts light on the temptation stories. What Jesus resisted was the temptation to fulfil current expectations. Though based originally on Old Testament prophecies, those ideas were by that time more dependent on 'popular paperbacks' of the period. King Messiah was presented as organising a great banquet, standing on the temple pinnacle to announce the redemption of Israel, and bringing the nations under his heel. Satan urged Jesus to manipulate those expectations—and Jesus refused.

God is not a fairy godmother waiting in the wings to countersign every bright idea. He has a will of his own. He is Lord.

Faith Is Not the Opposite of Doubt

Because we often think it is, we unnecessarily flog ourselves (or allow enthusiasts to flog us). Faith is the opposite of *unbelief*. Doubt (as we have seen) is the stage between the two where we are, as yet, undecided as to which we will pursue. Poor 'doubting Thomas' took too long to decide (John 20:24–29). 'Stop doubting and believe,' was the tense prescription for him (27). He already had every inducement to commit himself to a resurrected Saviour. He had spent three years in Jesus' company, listened to the most profound explanation of death and resurrection, and now had eye-witness accounts from the people he knew best. What more could he ask? He was not rebuked for wanting to weigh the evidence, but for wanting too much to weigh.

So Thomas decided which way to jump...with a vengeance. He was the first to actually take on his lips the awesome assertion that this death-conquering man is *God*. 'Thomas answered, "My Lord and my God"' (28). Is that a clue to his previous hesitation? Did he see more clearly than the other disciples the implications of what he was invited to believe? Was the source of his doubt a perceptive realisation of what was involved in believing? Two other incidents in his life could suggest that.

A few weeks earlier, the disciples were in a typically euphoric mood, quite unable to grasp the implications of Lazarus' fatal illness and the astonishing claims that Jesus was making about its outcome.

> 'Our friend Lazarus has fallen asleep; but I am going there to wake him up.'
>
> His disciples replied, 'Lord, if he sleeps, he will get better.' Jesus had been speaking of his death, but his disciples thought he meant natural sleep.
>
> So then he told them plainly, 'Lazarus is dead...but let us go to him.'
>
> Then Thomas said to the rest of the disciples, 'Let us also go, that we may die with him.'
>
> (John 11:11–16)

Most commentators give Thomas stick for being 'doubtful and despondent'. But was he? He saw *far more* than the others how a staggering new miracle three miles outside Jerusalem at the time of Passover would inevitably lead to a confrontation with the authorities and to Jesus' death. He was right (11:45–50). What is his reaction? 'I'm ready to go with him, and if necessary die with him.' Neither doubt nor despondency here, but a grim wrestling with reality, and a decision to commit himself regardless.

The other incident comes a few days later, and under the shadow of Jesus' impending death. Peter, euphoric once again, is promising to lay down his life for him (13:36–39). Jesus speaks somewhat elliptically of preparing a place and opening a way (14:1–4). Again, it is Thomas who tries to get to the depths of what Jesus is saying. 'Thomas said to him, "Lord, we don't know where you are going, so how can we know the way?"' (14:5). He, at least, understands that they don't understand. It is to that honest question that Jesus gives a reply that has echoed through the centuries: 'I am the way and the truth and the life. No one comes to the Father except through me.' An answer to unbelief and despondency? No, an answer to a genuine struggle to get to the heart of the truth and its implications.

Doubt, then, is not the opposite of faith, but the central point between belief and unbelief, commitment and rejection. Take the analogy of *fear*. This is often supposed to be the opposite of courage. But, in actual fact, fear stands balanced between courage and cowardice. The question is, what do I *do* with my fear—something courageous or something cowardly? So doubt often stands undecided between faith (with all its demands) and unbelief (with all its consequences), and has to decide between the two. What shall I do with the arguments for and against; the price that demands to be paid; the implications which I suspect are greater than anyone has warned me. What shall I do with my own fears and feelings?

I have just heard a very moving testimony from a Chinese-Malaysian Christian. He was reared in a Buddhist extended family of about 40 individuals, under the firm rule of grandmother and father. Through attending a group Bible-study, he became a Christian. Should he declare the fact? He did so, and created a major crisis in the family, with grief, tears, appeals to ancestral values and family authority all pitted against him. He persevered with his Christian living, but for the moment he put off baptism because that would cause 'loss of face' to the parents—a grave hurt in Chinese culture. In time, two younger brothers were also converted and a vital change in all three of their characters was acknowledged by the family. Baptism was now acceptable, and he took the step. Years later he felt the call of God to Bible College and pastoral ministry. With the father due for retirement and younger brothers still being educated, this meant that he, the only breadwinner, might be unable to give financial support to the family. Tears and pleading followed once more. He agreed to put off the decision until God showed alternative provision for the family. When it began to arrive, in the form of regular anonymous gifts, he went ahead with Bible training. In the next few years he saw his grandmother, father and mother, brothers and sisters converted, and the idols removed from the household. To me, this is a magnificent story of faith, with valid doubt playing its healthy part at certain points. Here was a man who moved forward in God's will, at God's pace, pausing at each point to weigh the consequences.

The Nature of Saving Faith

So much for the negatives. Now for some positives. What is *faith*? What is *saving* faith—that irreducible minimum without which it is impossible to begin living in the single-mindedness of faith rather than the double-mindedness of doubt?

Enthusiastic evangelism has not always served us well here. Illustrations of sitting on a chair (you just believe it will hold you up, and sit on it) or climbing on a bus (the destination board says where it is going; it holds many other people, so get on board) often helpfully underline the need for decisive commitment, but badly underrate some of the other elements involved in believing in Christ for salvation.

Every pastor and leader has had to cope with people back from a high-pressure decision-making event (rally, conference, holiday or camp). Words of assurance have been put into their mouths, but they have only the haziest ideas of what they believe. Some then turn out well. God is both sovereign and gracious. His capacity for touching lives and reaching hearts is unlimited in its variety and condescension. He saw potential discipleship in Zacchaeus the quisling conman, Simon the urban terrorist, Mary Magdalene in whom were seven devils, and Saul of Tarsus who ran Jerusalem's KGB. He goes on seeing the possibilities in an extraordinary variety of people today. Watching him work is a delight; working with him is a breathtaking privilege. This is one of the real struggles for earnest Christians in days of 'renewal'. God insists on breaking into people's lives, free of the time-honoured traditional channels on which we have depended for the last 70 years.

Nevertheless, far too many of our hopeful new converts make a few weeks' progress, and then come to a halt, or simply disappear from view. Christianity has been added to the list of things they have 'tried'. Had they ever really started? Was there ever the essential minimum of faith in the first place? What kind of faith foundations make the essential minimum?

The New Testament's 'portrait-gallery of faith' (see Hebrews 11) gives what at first sight is a disarmingly simple definition. 'Without faith it is impossible to please God, because anyone who comes to him must believe that he exists and that he rewards those who earnestly seek him' (Heb 11:6). In fact there is a great deal in that. 'God exists' implies that he *is* what he himself declares himself to be—not a product of our own imagination (God in man's image) but revealed to those who seek him on his terms.

The illustrations then invoked by the writer involve a good deal more than sitting in a chair or climbing on a bus. We are introduced to people who defied popular opinion, went out on a limb in obedience to God, stood up against tyrants, refused to be misled by appearance, trusted God when there were no precedents, and were unshaken when things failed to go their way. It is time to examine in more detail what that kind of faith involves, for only such a faith will survive the corrosion of creeping doubt.

Note

[1] Helmut Thielicke, *Between God and Satan* (Baker Book House: USA, 1980), p 66.

Chapter 7

Foundations for Faith

I often use a cartoon film-strip on the introductory evening of a discipleship class or nurture group. It examines the great affirmation, 'I believe in God.'

A man stands in church, reciting these first words of the Creed. The balloon above his head reveals the subject of his actual thoughts…a set of golf-clubs. The equivalent for his wife is a pan boiling over on the gas stove. What does their belief in God actually mean?

Next picture shows a parrot in a cage. Instead of 'pieces of eight' or 'pretty Polly,' he has learned to say, 'I believe in God.' But does he really?

Here is a pantomine devil, with red tights, horns and pitchfork. He too says, 'I believe in God.' Really? Yes… 'You believe that there is one God. Good! Even the demons believe that—and shudder' (James 2:19).

Inadequate faith soon finds its foundations tested and shaken by the inevitable experiences of life. One of two things may happen. A mere Jesus-flavoured credulity will be discarded, and the ex-believer will disappear back into the unbelieving world. Alternatively, a time of testing and maturing will come, during which doubt and questioning become tools in the building of a better foundation for faith. For such a faith, certain ingredients in larger or smaller proportions are essential.

Help Me

Faith means discovering my helplessness. 'Nothing in my hand I bring,' said the old hymn-writer. That creates problems! There is a pharisee in us all. Once we turn (reluctantly) to some thoughts of God, our natural first instinct is to give him something and put him in our debt. But God, by definition, needs nothing. We are the needy.

Helplessness before God includes the inability to find him or to please him. *Truth revealed* is the answer to the first; *redemption achieved* is the answer to the second. God, the Bible tells us, has shown us what we could never discover for ourselves, and done for us what we could never achieve for ourselves—at the Cross.

That is why what passes for 'scholarly doubt' often does go hand-in-hand with ignorance of God's salvation. It sounds like a bit of terrible evangelical intolerance and bigotry to suggest that religious scholars who write doubt-promoting theology actually need to be born again. But that is often their own confession. A useful test of any acclaimed new theology is, 'Can it be preached in the form of a saving gospel message to ordinary people?'

Now of course not every new convert will put it in clear words from day one. But the lesson will have to be learned sooner or later. I have seen some hopeful starters simply take their faith off like a discarded jacket and walk away when some circumstance has arisen that demands a helpless, dependent relationship with God. This is not what they expected. Others have gone through painful readjustment and come out with faith stronger and more wholesome: 'So this is what trusting God really means!'

Forgive Me

Faith means admitting my guilt. Not only am I helpless; it is my fault. The person who says, 'Nothing in my hand I bring' must also say, 'Foul, I to the fountain fly, wash me, Saviour, or I die.' For my hands are not only empty; they are dirty.

Is 'conviction of sin' an essential prerequisite to conversion, as our evangelical forefathers often asserted? If that means coming in tears of contrition, or with a deep sense of the fear of judgement, I don't think we can insist on it right away. Repentance often *follows* conversion, as the now enlightened conscience begins to realise just what is involved in knowing a holy God. But we will never make much progress in the life of faith until we grasp that we have no rights, and that God is in no way obliged to save us. That is the whole danger of a blessing-centred evangelism that merely offers advantages and incitements. 'Come to God, and he will meet your needs,' is a true but wholly inadequate statement. It needs to be balanced with, 'Flee to God from your own sin, which angers him.'

This is important if we are to cope with a certain kind of doubt when it appears, as it most assuredly will. 'Why is God letting me hurt? Why hasn't God answered my prayer? Why doesn't God do what I want?' But he has not the slightest obligation. My obligation is to find what he wants and how he is achieving it. That includes his making me holy—no matter what it costs him and costs me.

You Are What You Say You Are

Faith means letting God be himself. The Bible claims to present a coherent and consistent account of who God is and how he acts. Genuine faith, to have any meaning and reality, must depend on that revelation. The convert to Christianity needs to have some concept of the facts about God. Otherwise, 'Unable to see God as he is, he cannot trust him as he should.'[1]

Some people will find that revelation hard to accept. Their reaction may be emotional, intellectual or philosophical. Often the 'How can God allow this?' kind of problem (deeply felt—I'm not disparaging it) springs from an inadequate view of God. If I have been led to believe in the Santa Claus idea of God (constantly busy with a bag full of goodies) then sooner or later I am going to be torn with doubt or tripped over by disillusionment when some goodie doesn't arrive or something painful does.

This is why a distressing period of 'doubt' may turn out to be enriching and fortifying in the long run. If it explodes inadequate and less than biblical ideas of God, the doubter will one day rejoice in his discovery of who and what God really is. This is what older theologians meant by the 'sovereignty of God'. One of them, Arthur Pink, puts it well:

> The sovereignty of God is something more than an abstract principle which explains the rationale of the Divine government: it is designed as a motive for godly fear, it is made known to us for the promotion of righteous living, it is revealed in order to bring into subjection our rebellious hearts. A true recognition of God's sovereignty humbles as nothing else does or can humble, and brings the heart into lowly submission before God, causing us to relinquish our own self-will and making us delight in the perception and performance of the Divine will.[2]

These Are the Facts

Faith means seeing and knowing. One of the silliest and commonest ideas today is that *faith* and *fact* are somehow supposed to be mutual enemies. Some years ago, Magnus Magnusson, the television presenter, was reproached for undermining traditional faith in the Old Testament story. He blandly replied that he was only handling archaeological facts, whereas 'religion is a matter of faith, not facts.' He had fallen into two cardinal errors.

First, he apparently imagined that he was handling 'pure facts'. Actually, archaeology is a combination of insufficient facts, partially destroyed evidence, interpretations and theories. But neither theology nor archaeological theory is a matter of pure facts. The archaeological theory claims to be no more than that—*theory*. I myself have seen two different archaeologists interpret a discovery as a first-century temple dungeon and a fifth-century cheese factory, and another object as either Joshua's altar or a watchtower from the time of Isaiah!

Second (and more seriously), he apparently thought that faith has nothing to do with facts. In reality, faith is a decision as to what to do with facts—how to interpret them and how to act on them. Faith is not less than fact, but more. Take another illustration from archaeology. It is a well established fact that late in the Bronze Age in the Middle East, Semitic invaders conquered parts of Canaan and changed its culture. *Faith* interprets that and avows that God made a covenant with Abraham and his descendants which gave them a Law to keep, a land to live in, and a promise to be fulfilled in Christ. But, of course, if the conquest of Canaan was not a historical fact in the first place, then there is nothing to make a faith statement about.

Faith speaks *from* facts and *to* facts. Therefore faith requires at least a minimum of facts. That is why Paul argues strenuously for the fact of the resurrection of Jesus, quoting eye-witnesses and offering his own testimony (I Cor 15:1–7). To this he adds the statement of faith, 'By this gospel you are saved,' and 'Christ died for our sins' (2, 3).

So a fundamental ingredient of faith is some knowledge of what I believe and why I believe it. 'Christianity invites people to an examined faith. Although a Christian should believe simply, he should not "simply believe".'[3]

The Bible nowhere (that I can think of) encourages 'blind faith'. On the contrary, it tells us repeatedly that unbelievers are blind and that believers have begun to 'see'. 'For God, who said, "Let light shine out of darkness," made his light shine in our hearts to give us the light of the knowledge of the glory of God' (II Cor 4:6).

Sometimes that 'answer' will need to be addressed to our own inward being when questions arise and doubts dismay. This is why the kind of popular apologetics so skilfully handled by Michael Green and the late David Watson have done such immense good in our generation. A good pastor-preacher will ensure that at least once a year his church will hear a series of sermons which outline what the gospel says and why we believe it.

I Commit Myself

Faith means self-surrender. John's Gospel has always been the favourite of evangelists and apologists who take their appeals and arguments to the real people 'out there'. I have handed out hundreds of copies of this Gospel at fairgrounds, factory gates, racecourses and market-places. I have had dozens of letters from those who eventually came to faith as a result of reading it. The choice may seem a strange one, since John is by far the most profound of the Gospel writers, and his work full of elliptical reasoning. But there are two reasons for the choice: John deliberately and confessedly writes to produce faith, selecting his material to that end (John 20:30–31); and he constantly uses phrases, anecdotes and illustrations which hammer away at the need for decisive commitment. The refrain rings out of every word-picture of Jesus. He is the Bread of Life, but bread must be eaten. He is the Living Water, but water must be drunk. He is the Good Shepherd, who invites us to follow him. He is the Door, and we must choose to enter. One particularly rich verse says it repeatedly, 'I am the bread of life. He who comes to me will never go hungry, and he who believes in me will never be thirsty' (6:35).

A fundamental of saving faith is the personal handing over of life, its decisions and destiny, to Jesus Christ. We are not saved by the doctrine of the Atonement, but by Jesus himself. When faith comes under fire, that commitment is tested.

Now I'm Sure

Faith involves some certainty. Christians have often argued as to whether certainty is an essential product of faith. If I do not *know* I am saved, have I no saving faith? On the one hand, the New Testament certainly sounds a note of glad assurance. Christians do not *hope* to reach heaven, or *try* to join God's family, or struggle for their salvation. Christ's work is complete, and we can know it.

On the other hand, the basis of that certainty is not quite as simple as it is sometimes made to sound in the evangelistic enquiry room. The oft-quoted fifth chapter of I John says a good deal more than 'he who has the Son has life' (12).

Leave the Holy Spirit room to build firm within the convert's heart a solid assurance based on the whole work of the Trinity (which is what that chapter really says). Don't put words of premature certainty on his lips. Ponder on the plain statistical fact that many who were taught to say, 'I know I have eternal life,' have subsequently proved that they had nothing of the sort. Then what was their assurance if not a false one inadequately based?

Yet true certainty can be hindered by all kinds of factors. Health, personality, theological stance...all of these can affect the feeling of certainty. Strict Baptists in rural England and Calvinists in the Scottish Highlands will often display a life and a faith that make it obvious to any onlooker that they are God's people, and yet fail to be sure of it themselves because of a particular theory of election. And every pastor knows how depression or the menopause can temporarily rob a Christian of the assurance once known. Then is assurance not a necessary part of faith after all? In essence, it is. Logically it should be, but subjectively it is not always. But at the very least, some understanding of the basis of certainty is a vital part of faith. This is where nurture groups and church membership classes come into their own.

Small Profits, Quick Returns

It becomes apparent that those helpful little illustrations of sitting in a chair and climbing on a bus are rather less than adequate as expressions of faith. Yet there is a simplicity in saving faith. It really is like a child putting his hand into his father's. People really do have the experience of waking up one morning as unbelievers and going to sleep that night as convinced Christians. My father was converted the very first time he ever heard the gospel. What is more, he only heard it because he lost his way to a political meeting and finished up in the wrong building. I can certainly name the evening I found Christ. It was preceded not by a period of gradual moving towards him but by a period of struggling against him. Or was that the same thing? 'It is hard for you to kick against the goads' (Acts 26:14). My father's experience and mine were equally real.

Over a long ministry, from observation and involvement with hundreds of individual conversions, I have, however, slowly come to the conclusion that evangelicals have caused a lot of problems with 'sudden conversion'. We believe in it, want very much to see it, and in our zeal sometimes manipulate people prematurely into it. In our anxiety to obtain a quick return we often get very small profit.

People have sometimes commented on an apparent contradiction between my public preaching and my personal counselling. In the first I expound glorious Bible texts that make sweeping statements. The completeness of Christ's work for us, the assurance of eternal life, the challenge to decisive commitment, the change in lifestyle that the Holy Spirit produces— these are my regular themes. I often illustrate them with the classic conversion stories of Christian history—Paul, Justyn Martyr, Augustine, St Francis, Martin Luther, Thomas Bilney, John Bunyan, John Wesley, Charles Spurgeon—and with anecdotes of contemporary conversions. All of this gives the impression (apparently...I don't mean it to be so) that the normal conversion is sudden, rapid, easily marked on the calendar, and 100% effective.

Yet when the same hearers come to talk to me privately, it sounds different. I patiently listen to all kinds of reservations, doubts and difficulties. I try to lay a foundation of facts and Scriptures over a period of weeks. I urge consideration of what conversion will involve. I avoid putting words of certainty into their mouths. I silently recall (they don't know this bit) the advice of a wise evangelist 15 years older than me. 'Teach them that Christ died for the world's sins. But don't teach them to say "Christ died for me." When the Holy Spirit teaches them that, you will know that his work is done.' Sometimes I will say, after several interviews, 'We've gone as far as we can go in discussion; there's nothing more for you to learn until you start to believe. Let me know when you do.' Sometimes my visitor will turn up happily and announce that he has come to faith since last week.

Why this apparent contradiction between sudden conviction and growing faith?[4] Surely it is the contrast between objective fact and subjective experience. The facts of God's grace, God's sovereignty, Christ's atonement, Holy Spirit regeneration, Bible promises —all of these are sharply defined, sharply presented, vividly portrayed. Everyone stands in God's sight either condemned or justified, either spiritually dead or quickened. But how those facts are brought to bear on the individual life, and how he comes into the awareness of being justified and quickened—that is a different matter. It varies as people vary. There is no boring repetitiveness in the way God works. Jesus warned us of that. 'The wind blows wherever it pleases. You hear its sound, but you cannot tell where it comes from or where it is going. So it is with everyone born of the Spirit' (John 3:8).

Those classic conversions illustrate both points. In fact, they were not really as sudden as our dramatic pulpit shorthand suggests. Saul of Tarsus struggled against growing evidence long before he had his Damascus Road encounter. Martin Luther wrestled for years with the question of pardon and assurance. John Bunyan drove himself and his wife distracted with swings of conviction and incredulity. John Wesley formed his Holy Club, and even crossed the Atlantic on religious endeavour, long before his heart was strangely warmed in Aldgate Street. Our sense of the dramatic and our appreciation of the truth combine to make some moment of decision or certainty symbolic of the whole process, especially when it was encapsulated in a Bible verse, as it so often was:

'The just shall live by faith' (Martin Luther).

'Christ Jesus came into the world to save sinners' (Thomas Bilney and Hugh Latimer).

'I can do all things through Christ who strengthens me' (Oliver Cromwell).

'To the man who does not work but trusts God who justifies the wicked, his faith is credited as righteousness' (John Wesley).

'Look unto me and be ye saved' (Charles Spurgeon).

This is where God's truth and human perception meet. This is the point at which the Holy Spirit brings to conscious climax the long-drawn struggle of the soul. John Bunyan pictures it as the moment when Christian stands at the foot of the Cross, feels the cords that bound the burden to his back melt away, and sees the burden bouncing and rolling down the hill until it reaches the edge of an empty sepulchre, 'where it fell in and I saw it no more'. But it would certainly not be true to say he *felt* it no more. Bunyan's plain prose account of his own pilgrimage (*Grace*

Abounding to the Chief of Sinners) makes it painfully clear that there was never any such one-off never-needed-again experience of certainty. His allegory says it, too, for within a few pages Christian is struggling up Hill Difficulty, wrestling with Apollyon and even imprisoned in Doubting Castle. Objective truth and subjective experience are sometimes allies and sometimes rivals. The more we take our stand on the first, the less we shall be unduly deflated or unduly elated by the second.

Notes

[1] Os Guinness, *Doubt* (Lion Publishing: Tring, 1976), p 67.
[2] A W Pink, *The Sovereignty of God* (Banner of Truth: Edinburgh, revised 1961), p 123.
[3] Guinness, *op cit*, p 82.
[4] For a full explanation of the various roads to conversion, see *Entering the Kingdom* (Monica Hill, editor. MARC Europe: London, 1986).

Chapter 8

Job and the Trial of Faith

Most Christians know about Job. He was the man noted for his patience. Rather fewer Christians have read right through the book that bears his name. Those who have often feel a rather furtive sense of disappointment. They seem to have missed something. Not to put too fine a point on it, they can't identify the answer to the book's question. For one thing, Job's proverbial patience is not immediately obvious. He curses the day he was born, complains of bitterness of soul, calls his well-meaning friends miserable comforters, and asks if their long-winded speeches will ever end.

It is also slightly disconcerting to wade through a lengthy book at the centre of the Bible only to be told at the end that much of it is nonsense that displeases God (42:3–7). The puzzle is multiplied by the marvellous poetry that keeps breaking through. Do real people actually talk like that? Why do they all speak in blank verse of the same quality and style? Why do they all sound like characters in a particularly lyrical passage of Shakespeare?

In fact, that last point may provide a useful clue. King Henry V of England really did live, and really did lead his yeoman-archers to an amazing victory over the French. In all likelihood he made encouraging sounds to his troops before battle. But of course he didn't really say, 'Once more into the breach dear friends, once more. Or fill the walls up with your English dead.' Shakespeare has 'worked up' the facts into poetic and dramatic dialogue. That is perfectly legitimate; it is what the writer of the play is supposed to do. It may well be that God has chosen in his wisdom (when giving us the Book of Job) to inspire it in that style, just as he inspired Moses to write legislation, David to write songs, Isaiah to write poetry, Paul to write letters and John to write an apocalypse—all well-known literary devices. The Bible is the richer and we are the better for them. Truth, then, is much more than the recital of facts, just as wisdom is more than the accumulation of knowledge. There are times when straight prose is a poor vehicle for communicating truth, for the depths of truth may be too personal, too sensitive, too dynamic to be reduced to a drab recounting of externally perceived events. Job takes us deeper.

Debate in Heaven and Disaster on Earth

The 'prologue' is perhaps the book's strangest feature. We eavesdrop on a debate around the throne of God in which Satan challenges the possibility of genuine disinterested love for God. How much of this, again, is a literary device? What is quite certain is the reality of hell's accusation and the reality of heaven's permission in any balanced view of human suffering. As the story continues, the accuser is allowed to stretch Job's patience, faith and fortitude to breaking-point.

One calamity after another falls on unfortunate Job. Wealth, family and health are snatched from him. Added to his misfortune is the well-intentioned but maladroit counsel of his friends. They are thoroughly 'orthodox' as far as they go, but they goad Job into a frenzy of argument and despair.

I recall rereading this book during a period of rapid

growth in my church. People flowed in, bringing their problems and situations with them. Some of our traditional members began to suspect (with justification) that I was not invariably greeting these people with a no-nonsense black-and-white biblical proof-text of the 'get right or get out' variety. I tried, then, to explain my approach in a church magazine article that referred to Job's disappointing friends, showing that dogmatism won't do today. People's problems are too real, too human, too intense. To those who need our help, a snap text from the Bible, divorced from either its own context or the person's real life, just will not do. How fond we are of our proof-texts! How completely they freeze on my lips when I confront a man whose sin cannot be undone, a girl who cries, 'Mr Bridge, I just cannot', a keen mind that jibs at swallowing unproven assertions, a child whose parents have cruelly betrayed him, a woman struggling with bereavement.

Not an Answer, But a Vision

'Then the Lord answered Job out of the storm' (38:1). It is with some relief that the persevering reader reaches this point. Answers at last! But a first reading is likely to produce a sense of disappointment. It isn't an answer at all. Or at any rate it is only a response to Job's bitterest complaint, not an answer to the question, 'Why suffering?' No solutions are suggested. No hint of Satan's contribution is offered. Instead, the reader is offered a conducted tour of the created world, with hints of the bigger universe. Thunderstorms and blizzards, star-spangled sky and blazing sunrise (38), an ordered universe from day one of creation (39), wild beasts and domestic animals (40)... what is this? Marvellous, evocative poetry, but how is that supposed to answer the problem of Job's agony (Stephen's martyrdom, William Cowper's insanity, David Watson's death)? What has that to say to Dachau, Hiroshima, Ethiopia, the Gulag Archipelago?

These closing chapters, in fact, provide not an answer but a vision. Job grasps that, for his response is, 'I spoke of things I did not understand...My ears had heard of you but now my eyes have seen you' (42:3, 5). In other words, I looked for understanding, but what I have found is something better—a satisfying view of God to which I submit my pain.

In fact the vision of God does several things.

It highlights Job's limited viewpoint

Bound by both time and space, what hope has he of seeing whole the giant purposes of God? 'Where were you when I laid the earth's foundation?' (38:4). Sorry, not present at the time. 'Have you journeyed to the springs of the sea...(and) comprehended the vast expanses of the earth?' (38:16, 18). Well no, not exactly. Half of the problem is simply that we can't see far enough.

It enforces God's control of all events

The sea scared ancient Jews. It seemed to represent everything that is threatening, immense, unpredictable and uncontrollable. But God knows what he's doing with it. 'This far you may come and no farther; here is where your proud waves halt' (38:8–11). Dare we believe he says the same to the incoming tide of trial and temptation? Paul would believe it in a later day (I Cor 10:13).

It acknowledges the explicable and the inexplicable in every event

'You see the phenomenon of light and darkness, snow and rain, constellations wheeling through vast space, and a land alive with animals—but who gives the orders?' That is the gist of chapter 38 (see 5, 12, 28, 34). Incidentally, modern science with its talk of natural laws only puts the question one step back. If there are laws, who is the lawgiver?

What is God Saying, Then?

God says something like this: 'Job, you are looking for reasons. You have suggested to me in your agony that you could make a better job of things than I do. Well, until you know a little more about how to run the material universe (the easy bit) perhaps you should lay off telling me how to run the moral and spiritual universe?'

That is what makes Job's final response so magnificent (42:1–6). 'Now I understand.' (What? What's the secret I still haven't seen?) 'Now I understand that you, God, understand what I don't understand.' As simple and as bald as that. The modern reader of the book ought to have seen it sooner. He has read the first two chapters, and Job hasn't. Indeed, the whole point of the first two chapters would be lost if Job *could* read them. Satan has been at work. God's glory has been impugned. The assertion has been made that genuine love for God doesn't exist. People only put into religion for what they get out of it. God says, 'Not so,' and Job's terrible experience begins.

It is rather like reading an Agatha Christie for the second time. *Now* you can see the vital clues in the first couple of chapters. I always find it more enjoyable the second time round. Of course!

Pain or Faith on Trial?

That raises a fundamental question about the whole Book of Job. We usually think of it as a book about suffering. But is it? Not really. Suffering is a vital ingredient in the story, but it is no more a book about suffering than Mark's Gospel is a book about Galilee. Job is a book about *faith*, specifically, faith's reaction and faith's response to the test that suffering brings to it. Seen that way, the whole perspective shifts. It doesn't even attempt to answer the question, 'Why does a world run by God feel pain?' It poses the question, 'How should a person of faith respond when pain comes?'

Now we see a lot of suggestions. Naïve, simplistic equations of personal sin and personal suffering don't add up. Equally simplistic equations of faith with health and prosperity don't add up either. Miracles and spooky experiences don't provide an answer. A lot of facts come into the real equation which the sufferer can't see, such as Satan's activity, God's wider purpose, and life beyond the grave.

We see some surprising and comforting facts, too. God doesn't rebuke Job for his wild, despairing outbursts and raging doubts. He does rebuke Job's well-meaning friends for their shallow 'answers'. The Lord said to Eliphaz, 'I am angry with you and your two friends, because you have not spoken of me what is right' (42:7).

Angry with them? But were they not trotting out the kind of success formulae that can be built up from a few well chosen texts? God does say 'angry'!

In fact, God says Job should pray and offer sacrifices for the men who proferred their Faith Formulae (42:8–9). Now there's a thought. One consequence of the godly suffering is that they will be able to minister sympathetically to their friends when *they* suffer—as Paul says at some length (II Cor 1:3–7).

So, it is faith that is on trial in this book, not pain. It is very understandable, but rather peculiarly modern, that suffering should be seen as a problem to faith. Being modern myself, I see it that way. But as a famous apologist has pointed out, every great religious movement known was initiated before the invention of anaesthetic. Ancient man's problem was not 'Why does God treat me so badly?' but rather, 'What possible inducement could I produce to persuade God to treat me better than I deserve?' John Newton, the eighteenth-century slave-captain turned saintly preacher, when confronted by the likelihood of a painful death for his deeply-loved wife, commented, 'As a sinner I cannot complain, and as a saint I will not question.' The peculiarly modern custom of putting God in the dock as someone not coming up to expectation is often exposed by C S Lewis:

> The ancient man approached God as the accused person approaches his judge. For the modern man the roles are reversed. He is the judge; God is in the dock...if God should have a reasonable defence for being the god who permits war, poverty and disease, he is ready to listen to it...But the important thing is that man is on the bench and God in the dock.[1]

The patience of faith

This is the place to which Job's faith eventually takes him. He has got very near at times to putting God on trial. 'Why is life given to a man...whom God has hedged in?' (3:23). 'What have I done to you?' (7:20). Strong stuff. I sometimes say to people bitterly hurt and tending to moan, 'If you *have* to moan (and sometimes we all have to), then moan to God; the psalmist often did.' And I show them a few examples. Reading them aloud can do a world of good. But in the end Job's faith brings him through moving hints of dependence upon God and confidence in redemption beyond the grave, to the point of surrender to God's superior wisdom. I don't understand; you do; it is too wonderful for me to understand (42:1–6). The question 'Why suffering?' remains noticeably unanswered. The question 'What is faith?' finds a glorious answer: 'Faith is surrender to God.' That is why the New Testament sees Job, in spite of his occasional outbursts, not as a man who solved the enigma of pain, but a man who showed patient, steadfast faith (James 5:10–11).

British television featured in 1985 a vivid illustration of Job's experience. The poignant film *Shadowlands* retold the story of C S Lewis, the great Christian apologist, and his romance with Joy Davidman. The long-time bachelor found love of a rare kind in his brief marriage to one of his own converts. She was seriously ill with cancer when they married, but after receiving the laying-on of hands in hospital experienced a remarkable remission of the disease. Two years of bliss followed. Then the cancer struck back savagely, and Joy died in great pain. Lewis's grief was inconsolable. Friends who tried to comfort him with reflections of his own teachings were told, 'It just won't do.' The man who had given faith and solace to thousands could find none for himself...for a while.

Gradually, however, he found peace again. The shadows receded. Books such as *Letters to Malcolm* and *A Grief Observed* show how he managed to cling to faith and sanity. One feature was a significant change in a position he had previously held as a Christian. Years earlier, *The Problem of Pain* (1940) had touched on an old but complicated philosophical chestnut. Is something 'right' because God says it is, or does God say it is right because it is? The orthodox answer is usually taken to be the former. Absolute standards are defined by an absolute lawgiver. If it were the other way round, 'right' would be more absolute than God himself. He would be getting his standards from somewhere else, so to speak. He would be in a sense dependent.

But God's glory is his absolute independence. He needs nothing (Acts 17:25). Everything and everyone needs him and draws its existence and definition from him. Lewis had indeed expressed that fact powerfully and lucidly.

> God has no needs...God is Goodness. He can give good, but cannot need it or get it...The freedom of God consists in the fact that no cause other than himself produces his acts...his own goodness is the root from which they grow and his own omnipotence the air in which they flower.[2]

But that made it very difficult for Lewis to continue his argument at all. For an argument assumes some possibility of evidence and demonstration. So in that early book he still settled for a view of God as someone who accepts 'right' as an absolute fact outside of himself, which others can recognise. They can therefore say to themselves, 'However painful my present experience, however puzzling the facts, I can see that God is acting rightly, by a definition of rightness that I can grasp.'

So Lewis went on to argue in his powerful and effective way. But when—20 years later—the writer met his bitterest tragedy, these arguments that had helped so many did not help him. Or, at any rate, he came to change his view on that question of who defines good.

> He only succeeded in holding on to his faith by moving to the very position he had earlier rejected: 'things are right because God commands them'. That is faith's Everest. There, in Lewis's words, you will hear God's compassionate voice saying; 'Peace, child, you don't understand.' Or as Job put it at the end of the book that bears his name, 'I talked about things I did not understand, about marvels too great for me to know.' There, ultimately, the problem of pain is to be faced and coped with.[3]

With Friends Like This Who Needs Enemies?

This is much more than Job's friends can attain to. They try hard, but fail lamentably. Eliphaz bases his argument on *experience*. General observation of life (and a special private religious experience) leads him to the sweeping assertion that suffering is always the direct result of your own sin (chapters 4–5). It is the slick answer of the *moralist*. 'You shouldn't have done it in the first place. Our church has always frowned on that. Sorry, but you've got what you deserve.'

Bildad was different. He relied on too much *tradition*. 'As in the former generation' (8:8). It leads him to accuse Job of being a hypocrite. Our modern *legalist* still falls back too heavily on tradition, which can be found helpless in the face of new pressures, new problems and new cultures.

Zophar (chapter 11) is different again. He is the *dogmatist*. A good ticking-off, replete with sweeping generalisation and devoid of any reason, is his contribution.

Job's friends are satirically portrayed in all their pompous piety to expose facile philosophies. The resemblance both to orthodox traditionalism and to new radical faith-promoting formulae is striking and uncomfortable. The argument of *both* (expressed in very different ways) is summed up in the assertion that faith and virtue always pay. But they don't. Not here. It just won't wash. Consider two simple facts. Africa, the most 'Christian' continent on earth, is currently the hungriest. Arabia, one of the most aggressively anti-Christian, is the richest.

The Theology of Humpty Dumpty

I recently met a beaming, extrovert television preacher who achieved a remarkable volte-face with the Book of Job. He maintained that the three 'comforters' were right after all. What Job needed was a bit more faith and obedience. He ought to have got up and fought instead of lying down and letting it roll over him.

Arguing with him, I felt rather like Alice talking to Humpty Dumpty, who reserved the right to make any word mean anything he wanted it to mean. With remarkable dexterity, he made most of the things we admire about Job appear as weaknesses and vices—the fatherly prayer in chapter 1, for instance. I would have thought most parents seeing their teenagers off to a party would do the same, committing them anxiously in prayer. But no, this enthusiast assured me that

Job's fundamental fault comes out here. He said, 'Those were fear words, and they sprang from a heart of fear. Job should have said, "My sons are good sons and they know right from wrong. May God's blessing rest on them. Everything's gonna work out fine".'

I nervously suggested that Job's magnificent surrender to God's ways was a point in his favour. 'The Lord gave, and the Lord hath taken away; blessed be the name of the Lord' (1:21 AV). But not so, it seems. That's just typical of the way Job has misled thousands of Christians who lose a child or a life-partner, and quote these words for comfort. Job put the blame on God, but he shouldn't have done. It wasn't God who took his family, but the Devil. He went on, 'There's not a bit of faith in it. God isn't the killer. Satan's the killer. All this stuff about *though he slay me yet will I trust him*, brings tears to your eyes, doesn't it? But it's not true. *Satan* is the one who wants you dead. *He* is the one who kills people's babies.'

I gave up the discussion. God gave his own verdict on Job's specious 'comforters', and we can safely leave him to say the last word on this kind of thinking, too. For it goes even further than they went. Not only does it rob the suffering believer of his integrity and accuse him of unbelief; it draws a picture of a silent God and a Devil who almost always wins. The sovereignty of God—that supreme comfort of the saints—has no place here.

But it is precisely to that sovereignty that the Book of Job leads us. Before that point of submission is reached, Job is allowed to go to remarkable lengths in arguing with God. The same kind of experience is often illustrated in the Psalms (eg 10, 73, 74) for the same reason. God's sovereignty is the foundation fact of the universe, from which all other realities draw their very existence. It is the only foundation on which faith can build. A man or woman will not learn to stand on that foundation without facing some of the lesser realities in all their starkness, unimpressed by threadbare, escapist explanations. That is why a certain kind of questioning doubt is not sinful unbelief (to be rewarded with a reproving slap on the wrist) but an actual function of faith itself.

What Job Never Had

The modern Christian reaching the end of Job's book will still feel that there is more to be said. His instinct is correct. We can easily forget how little the Old Testament saints had because they did not have Jesus.

Job knew nothing of Satan's activity and Satan's defeat

We have to remember that Job never read the first two chapters of the Book of Job! He knew nothing of Satan's observation of him (1:7), Satan's challenge to his genuine piety (1:9), or God's permission to Satan to go so far in attacking him. There is little of this in the Old Testament. It is the New Testament that describes how 'the accuser of our brothers' accuses us before God 'day and night' (Rev 12:10). It is certainly only the New that tells us how that accuser has been 'hurled down (and) overcome...by the blood of the Lamb' (12:10–11).

Jesus has broken Satan's power. That is a glorious New Testament theme. By his death he has silenced the accusations made against us (Rom 8:33), delivered us from the fear of death that Satan once held over us (Heb 2:14–15), and disarmed the powers that pitted themselves against us and enslaved us (Col 2:14–15).

Job knew nothing of the Mediator whom God has provided

He sees *the need* for someone to stand half-way between God and man, making God's ways clear to bewildered people and conveying their frailties and feelings to God. 'If only there were someone to arbitrate between us, to lay his hand upon us both' (9:33). 'My intercessor is my friend as my eyes pour out tears to God; on behalf of a man he pleads with God as a man pleads for his friend' (16:20–21).

So he puts up his pathetic and moving pleas. His well-meaning friends don't know *him* for they make totally unjustified hints about bad motives and secret sins that are the product of their own inadequate explanations. And they certainly don't know *God*, because they completely fail to come to grips with the problem of what God is up to.

A mediator! The ancient pursuit of priests and the modern pursuit of psychologists and sociologists (both in vain) express the human longing for some go-between. In Jesus the Christian has that very sweet certainty. Faith takes hold of one who is able 'to sympathise with our weaknesses...tempted...yet without sin' (Heb 4:15). Faith enables us to say with confidence, 'There is one God and one mediator between God and men, the man Christ Jesus, who gave himself as a ransom for all' (I Tim 2:5).

Job knew nothing of life after death

Certainly he groped for it. Such a certainty would obviously cast the whole problem in a new light. He protests that the absence of such a certainty would make life meaningless. 'So he who goes down to the grave does not return...Therefore I will not keep silent'

(7:9–11). In one magnificent moment of faith he grasped it briefly.

> I know that my Redeemer lives, and that in the end he will stand upon the earth. And after my skin has been destroyed, yet in my flesh I will see God; I myself will see him with my own eyes...How my heart yearns within me.
>
> (Job 19:25–27)

But on the whole the certainty evaded him, as it did them all, until Jesus came and died and broke death's power by rising from the dead. It is the empty tomb that brings the certainty of life after death, not tales, however impressive, of people with near-death experiences who have been dragged back by modern medical skill. 'Christ has indeed been raised from the dead, the firstfruits of those who have fallen asleep' (I Cor 15:20). Faith grasps that, and says with ringing certainty, 'Because he lives, I shall live.' Suddenly the question of why unpleasant things happen has been put into a whole new dimension: the dimension of eternity. This is why Paul can say that his own severe sufferings were simply not worth comparing to the glory that would follow (II Cor 4:16–18).

Job knew nothing of the Holy Spirit

The Spirit was no stranger to this world in Job's day; he was seen as brooding over the face of the waters at the moment of Creation; he was known giving strength to Samson, passing prophecy to Saul, moving David to sing and Amos to warn and Isaiah to plead. But his *residence* amongst men was still future, promised but not seen by Joel and Jeremiah and Ezekiel.

Job never mentions him. Now to the Christian he is heaven's throne-gift, the family inheritance for every believer whom Jesus is not ashamed to own as younger brother and sister. He is here to stay, resident in the heart of each Christian. Again, it is faith that says that it is so, and faith that taps the resources that are now available. 'The Father...will give you another Counsellor to be with you for ever—the Spirit of truth...He lives with you and will be in you' (John 14:16–17). 'Having believed, you were marked...with a seal, the promised Holy Spirit' (Eph 1:13).

Job knew nothing of the fellowship of the Church

The nearest thing he got to it, I suppose, was the sympathetic silence with which his friends first reacted to his grief (2:11–13). It was a genuine contribution, but there was no follow-through, and little spiritual insight beyond the eloquent trotting-out of conventional religion.

But through faith in Christ, the believer now enters into the Household of Faith, the living Church made up of all those who share Christ's life. Christians are as close to each other as different limbs are in the same body (I Cor 12:12–20). For us, as for Job, there is no final answer to our doubts and no complete response to our cries, short of that future day when, 'I shall know fully, even as I am fully known' (I Cor 13:12). But the coming of Christ, with all that this set in motion, provides us with a magnifying glass through which we can see the partially understood with a new clarity.

Notes

[1] C S Lewis, *God in the Dock* (Collins/Fountain: London, 1982 reprint), p 100.
[2] C S Lewis, *The Problem of Pain*, 1940 (Collins/Fount: London, 1977 reprint), pp 23, 41.
[3] Morgan Derham, 'A Modern Job and his Message', *Scripture Union Daily Notes* (October–December 1986).

Chapter 9

Problems with Prayer

Have you ever paused in your prayers and felt it an exercise in futility? *What do I* imagine I'm doing? Here I am, kneeling on the carpet, my face stuck in the cushion of an armchair, talking to myself. Is something going to happen in China because I do this? What conceivable effect can this have on my aunt's X-rays?

Prayer offers more unanswerable questions than most topics. If God already has his plans, how can my prayer alter them? Why does he need to be told what he already knows? Why do I only sometimes get an answer? Why is prayer so *hard*?

God is very gentle with new Christians — have you noticed? He sometimes gives them immediate answers. Later on it doesn't happen nearly so often. The full truth about prayer is more complicated than we were first allowed to believe. After all, a child is permitted for a while to think that the sun rises, that Santa Claus brings presents, and that God lives in the sky. It does no harm, and a great deal of good. It is a preliminary process in learning the real facts about the solar system, father's wage-packet, and the transcendence of God.

A lonely friend of mine, in rather special circumstances, once prayed, 'God, if you are there, please give me a piano.' She found one on the doorstep 15 minutes later. It brought her to church next week, and to conversion within two months. Then she prayed for a husband, but it was a very long time before *he* turned up on the doorstep. Meanwhile, she had to learn quite painfully that she wanted a man much more than she wanted God.

A member of my congregation last week told me he came to Christ in sheer astonishment when his wife prayed to Christ for his broken-down car in a dangerous spot on a busy road—and it promptly worked. But he normally employs a garage mechanic.

I can recall, as a youth, explaining to a surprised church elder that I had noticed an almost exact mathematical equation between time spent in prayer and conversions through my preaching. It has not quite continued, but it was the means by which God introduced me to both activities.

No Easy Answers

Most of the general categories of doubt (Chapter 2) find their special place in the problems of prayer. *Emotion*: Often I don't *feel* like it. Disappointing answers get me down. *Intellect*: how can prayer achieve anything when we are assured we live in a closed system of measurable cause and effect? *Disillusionment*: either some enthusiast exaggerates their success stories, or it doesn't work for me. *Impatience*: nothing is more sensitive than the trusting-waiting-believing relationship of prayer. *Wrong motives*: see prayer as principally a means of getting things from God, and we will soon be thoroughly muddled.

Who's in Charge?

The mechanics of prayer are a problem on their own. What exactly is happening when I tell God something, or ask for his help? How does he do it? Presumably there are millions of other people asking as well. Am I to imagine the divine Mind processing every request, weighing its implications, reshuffling circumstances to meet it, and somehow squeezing the new scenario into line with all the other requests and all the other circumstances—like an infinite disc in an enormous computer? Someone has suggested that it is rather like an author planning the movements of characters in a book. But here are enough characters to make *War and Peace* look like a short story—and they keep coming alive and writing their own pages.

It certainly assumes a mind incredibly complex, and a power immense beyond imagining. That is exactly what we mean when we talk about omniscient omnipresence—in fact—God. We simply have to assert that God is such a Being by definition. Like our reply to the child who asks, 'If God made everyone, who made God?' to which we can only reply, 'The word "God" *means* someone who has always been there and had no beginning.'

Both are statements of faith. Atheists will find them irritating. But they themselves have to make even more unlikely faith statements. A mainstay of the atheistic view of the origin of the universe with all its apparent signs of order and planning is a completely unproven and unprovable assertion: 'Anything can happen by accident if you give it long enough.' The Christian prefers to believe that anything can happen by intention if you allow it an omniscient Creator.

Microchips and Miracles

Modern technology provides some interesting analogies. It is now easier than it used to be to imagine a mind of infinite wisdom combining and permutating millions of competing facts and circumstances. A computer does something quite like that. Of course, the computer does not actually initiate anything. But it does almost imitate one thing which we have to imagine God doing in response to millions of prayers.

Some Jews in modern Jerusalem engage in an

attractive piece of nonsense. They arrange to be buried after they die on the slopes of the Mount of Olives. When God sets up Judgement Day in that area, they reason, there could be a distinct advantage in being early on the scene. People well up in the queue may be able to present their alibis and excuses before the divine Judge gets too tired of listening to such things. But the computer explodes that vain hope. If an electronic gadget can marshall and print out our murky pasts in seconds, the process of judgement need not take long.

Nor need the process of weaving our prayers into a complete scheme. In the very moment that a missionary's car goes into a skid, God can hear the driver's split-second prayer and fit it into the whole scheme of things, including God's purpose for that Christian's life, for everyone else's life on the motorway, for the lives of those who built the road and the lives of ambulance attendants, doctors, nurses and firemen.

More than one answer

Consider that illustration further. Some answers must be 'negative' to make others positive. Certain answers are just not possible in the nature of things. They are moral or logical impossibilities. A teacher prays for sunny weather during the Sunday school outing. A farmer prays for badly needed rain on his crops. It is manifestly impossible for both of them to have what they ask in the same place, at the same time. C S Lewis writes:

> 'Nothing which implies contradiction falls under the omnipotence of God,' says Thomas Aquinas. 'God cannot do all things, because he cannot deny himself'

explains the Westminster Catechism. God's omnipotence means power to do all that is intrinsically possible, not to do the intrinsically impossible…You may attribute miracles to him, but not nonsense.[1]

So the permutations possible in God's answers to our prayer are not unlimited. Some are morally out of bounds. Some are intrinsically impossible. One assumes, with John Calvin, that the means God uses to influence his own creation varies with the nature of the thing he has created. The psalmist tells us that God makes the grass grow, but presumably not in the same way as he invites human beings to keep his commandments. God rules mineral life by physical laws, vegetable life by organic laws, animal life by that plus instinct, and human life by all that again, plus conscience, choice, intelligence. With Christians the mechanism is even more sensitive…something like partnership (though not *equal* partnership) now comes into it.

The power of choice

God wants friends, not robots. The awesome power of choice comes into the equation. So here is another complication. In the answering of my prayers, my own will and the wills of other people are involved. And some of them may have no desire to do God's will at all. Complicated.

Consider (with compassion) a Christian prisoner in some unspeakable Russian jail, ill-treated by a brutal prison guard. The Christian will pray for courage and patience, and will doubtless get it. He may well pray for the jailer to stop being so brutal. But the jailer has no desire to stop. Suppose God, in answer to prayer, *changes* the jailer. But the most likely way to achieve that (it has often happened in church annals) is to speak to his conscience through the suffering fortitude of the prisoner...which means the prisoner suffering long enough for the endurance to show.

Two Levels of Prayer

It is helpful to think of prayer at two levels. First-degree prayer is concerned with real basics. 'Show me your will.' 'Make me more like Jesus.' 'Help me to conquer my bad temper.' Usually we can be pretty sure of God's wishes at this level. We hardly need to add, '... if it be your will,' for he has declared his will in these matters.

Second-degree prayer is more concerned with details. Quite often its concern is for the specific fulfilment of a first-degree prayer. 'Show me your will in this morning's sermon.' 'Make me more like Jesus in my attitude to those neighbours.' 'Help me to conquer my bad temper through the laying-on of hands.' But that may not be God's way of achieving the objective. We are simply making a kind of reverent suggestion; this is how God might do it.

At its most basic level, a second-degree prayer is often simply a cry for help. 'Stop it hurting.' 'Help me catch that train.' 'Get me out of this.' But what if missing the train is God's way to teach me patience and get my temper under control (not by the laying-on of hands after all)? What if another prayer I prayed three days ago (Lord help me to witness to someone this week) is about to be answered while I sit in the waiting-room until the next train arrives—next to someone who has asked God to show her the way of salvation? Second-degree prayers are perfectly valid, but a lot less likely to be answered exactly the way we hope.

Years ago, my wife and I 'dedicated' our newborn sons to God in a simple church ceremony. Amongst several other prayers, we asked that they might come in due time to acknowledge Jesus as Lord in their lives. That was a first-degree prayer. As the years passed, we saw many ways in which that might possibly happen. We turned the possibilities into prayer. 'Lord, help that Sunday school teacher...' 'When Billy Graham comes to Newcastle...' 'That youth camp in August...' In the event, one son was converted at the youth camp and the other after a talk with his mother, following a sermon by his father. The basic prayer was happily answered; some of the secondary prayers were not God's way.

Here is a simple principle, then. Basic prayer requests are concerned with God's expressed will. Secondary prayers are concerned with the detailed fulfilment, or with matters where we do not have a clear Word from God. The faith required of the first is to take God at his Word. The faith needed in the second is to hold on and trust when we are not sure. If I insist on regarding secondary prayers as if they are basic prayers, I am bound to get disappointed and frustrated when the answer has to be 'No' because there is a better way.

A better answer

Church history provides a famous example. St Augustine of Hippo, fifth-century scholar and theologian, was in his youth a notorious libertine. His godly mother Monica prayed for his conversion and commitment to God's service. He determined to study philosophy in Rome. Monica was horrified. The teaching was pagan, the city was an open temptation to immorality. She pleaded with her son not to go, and with God to stop him. Neither plea was apparently heard. Augustine went to Rome, came under the influence of Bishop Ambrose, and committed his life to Christ. Monica's primary prayer was thus answered by the 'No' to her more detailed prayer.

Augustine enjoyed the divine humour and wisdom of it. 'In the depths of your wisdom, you heard the main point of her desire. You regarded not what she then asked, so that you might make me what she had always desired.'[2]

Praying for Our Families

The subject of prayer for our children is a sensitive one. Proverbs 22:6 is often quoted by grieving parents who are, frankly, whistling in the wind. Their children *have* 'turned from the way'. Did they, then, not 'train them'? Or does it count if the children yet come back in the future? Does God promise?

God's timetable is not always ours. Its climax (in some issue) may stretch beyond our life-span. How often I have introduced middle-aged people to Christ whose deceased parents or life-partner prayed for that outcome but did not live to see it.

I know of a remarkable incident. A seaman, much prayed for by Christian parents, was swept overboard in a storm. In the water, he cried to God to save his soul. The next wave swept him back on board, and he lived to prove his new-found faith. But if his life had not been spared, his parents would have thought for the rest of their lives that their prayers had not been answered. All the evidence would have suggested his impenitent death—and all the evidence would have been wrong.

May we imagine God saving up our prayers, so to speak? So stalwart a Puritan as Thomas Goodwin could write:

> There may be some prayers which you must
> be content never yourselves to see
> answered in this world, the accomplishing
> of them not falling out in your time...There
> is a common treasure of the church, not of
> their merits but of their prayers...what a
> collection of prayers hath there been these
> many ages.[3]

Partnership, Not Persuasion

Something vital still has to be said. The purpose of
prayer is not to persuade God to do anything, least of
all to change his mind. Prayer is an exercise in which
we get ourselves into the mind, motive and will of
God, and *co-operate with his purposes*. That principle
lies at the very heart of the Lord's Prayer: 'Your kingdom come, your will be done.' It broke from the tor-
tured lips of Jesus in Gethsemane: 'Not as I will, but as
you will' (Matt 26:39).

Prayer is co-operation with God. That key unlocks
the secret of Jesus' own great prayer-promises. They
seem to imply unlimited possibilities, yet at the same
time clear boundaries. Seeking first God's kingdom,
asking in Christ's name so that the Father is glorified,
asking whatever we wish because we abide in him; all
these phrases really ring the changes on one theme
(Matt 6:33; John 14:13–14; 15:7). They counter-
balance those other apparent blank-cheque promises
that require only faith. 'If you believe...', 'Whatever
you ask...', 'Believe that you have it...' (Matt 21:22;
Mark 11:24). We must ask, 'On what basis do I
believe?' The answer obviously is not just wishful
thinking. I believe because God has given me good

reason to think that this is his wish. God does not need to be persuaded to go my way; I must be persuaded to go his.

Why then pray at all, if the purpose of the exercise is God's will? One might as well ask, why *serve* God? The answer can only be: because it is my delight to do his will, and because he, in wonderful condescension, chooses to use both my prayers and my service for his own ends. Is that what Pascal meant when he said that God instituted prayer in order to lend his creatures the dignity of causality?

We have come round in full circle to the mystery of 'unanswered prayer'. There is no such thing. Every prayer of God's children is heard and answered. But the answer cannot always be 'Yes'. Cannot, because it is not his will. 'We, ignorant of ourselves, beg often our own harms, which the wise powers deny us for our good; so find we profit, by losing of our prayers.'[4]

Prayer is, above all else, communion with a person. Communion with any kind of person, our equal or inferior, is *per se* a good deal more than getting things off him. How much more so when the Person is infinitely, unimaginably, staggeringly superior to me in every way—when my whole life depends on the outflow of energy from that Person, and the only thing that really has any permanent significance is his opinion of me and his plan for me?

That is why *petition* (asking for things) is only a very small part of prayer—in a sense, the lowest part. It also includes confession and apology, gratitude and celebration, awe and worship, silence and contemplation, self-searching and readjustment, vision and intercession. I am communing with the Lord of Glory, not using a British Telecom answering-machine.

Prayer is request. The essence of request, as distinct from compulsion, is that it may or may not be granted. And if an infinitely wise Being listens to the requests of finite and foolish creatures, of course he will sometimes grant and sometimes refuse them. Invariable 'success' in prayer would not prove the Christian doctrine at all. It would prove something much more like magic.[5]

Notes

[1] C S Lewis, *The Problem of Pain*, 1940 (Collins/Fountain: London, 1977 reprint), pp 14, 16.
[2] Augustine, *Confessions*, Bk V 15.
[3] Iain Murray, *The Puritan Hope* (Banner of Truth: Edinburgh, 1971), pp 101–2.
[4] William Shakespeare, *Antony and Cleopatra*.
[5] C S Lewis, *Fern-seed and Elephants* (Collins/Fountain: London, 1976 edition), p 97.

Chapter 10

Fiery Darts and the Shield of Faith

What part does the Devil play in doubt? The existence of spiritual, personal evil is a sombre fact not to be dismissed lightly. In the preface to his great description of the armour of God, the apostle Paul warns that to see the battle in purely human terms is to miss a vital point. 'Our struggle is not against flesh and blood, but against the rulers, against the authorities, against the powers of this dark world and against the spiritual forces of evil in the heavenly realms' (Eph 6:12).

The charismatic movement has done the Church a service by recalling our attention to the subject. It is not saying anything new. Dr Martin Lloyd-Jones' massive series of sermons at Westminster Chapel, London, in the late 1950s, handled the subject in meticulous detail. His treatment bore many marks of William Gurnall's seventeenth-century classic *The Christian in Complete Armour*, a resource for Christian preachers ever since. (Eighteenth-century John Newton said that if he were only allowed one other book beside the Bible, he would choose this.) John Bunyan, that master-craftsman skilled at handling the human heart, often presented Christian experience in terms of satanic attack:

> Just when he was come over against the mouth of the burning pit, one of the wicked ones got behind him, and stepped up softly to him, and whispering, suggested many grievous blasphemies to him, which he

thought verily had proceeded from his own mind.[1]

An activity of demons? Dr Martin Lloyd-Jones thought so.

The Devil has often plagued some of the noblest saints with blasphemous thoughts… What the Devil hopes will happen is that the saint under attack will assume that they are his own thoughts and begin to doubt whether he is a Christian at all…The fiery darts.[2]

The Devil's Doubts

There are several reasons for supposing that Satan has a particular interest in the encouragement of doubt. He is called *the father of lies* (John 8:44), and false doctrine which undermines confidence in God's truth is attributed to demons (I Tim 4:1). Significantly, Satan's first activity described in the Bible is that of questioning the truth of God's Word (Gen 3:1). 'Did God really say…?' He is still at it.

In the context of a different kind of doubt, which undermines our sense of security in God's love, Satan is pictured as, 'the accuser of our brothers, who accuses them before our God day and night' (Rev 12:10). It is a picture vividly portrayed in the early chapters of Job, and in Zechariah's vision of 'Satan standing at his right side to accuse him' (Zech 3:1). Indeed, the words commonly translated 'Satan' and 'Devil' in Scripture mean literally 'accuser' and 'slanderer'.

Finally, it is suggestive that in Paul's description of

the armour of God, the shield of *faith* is employed to 'extinguish all the flaming arrows of the evil one' (Eph 6:16). (I have found it personally helpful, in times of conflict, doubt or fear, to engage in a prayer exercise in which I quietly and thoughtfully 'put on' each item of the armour. The mailed belt of truth, against lies and errors. The breastplate of righteousness against guilt for past sin and the power of present temptation. The sandals of peace, against temptations to complacency and defeatism in the battle for souls. The shield of faith against attacks on my confidence in God's Word and promises. The helmet of salvation, against mental distress and intellectual doubts. The sword of the Spirit, when engaged in applying Scripture to situations where faith quails and expectation runs low.)

No Demons Under the Bed

But a balance is necessary. Some well-meaning contemporary Christians have plunged into a demonology that goes beyond anything taught in the Bible. It can be as grotesque as the imaginations of the Middle Ages; unhealthy in emphasis and erratic to the point of eccentricity.

I am told by some enthusiasts that demons are the cause of practically everything. They fake medical symptoms of diseases that don't exist. They hide inside medicine that is taken in unbelief. When surgery is undertaken, they take the opportunity to move to another part of the body and fool everybody. They stop the flow of wealth that God wills for his people. They inhabit motor cars, machines and domestic animals. All this may be said with great sincerity, but it is a flirtation with *animism*. That most ancient and persistent form of paganism imagines that spirits inhabit and control all animate and inanimate objects. The job of the shaman (priest, witch-doctor) is to appease them, co-operate with them, or oppose them, as the circumstances require.

The danger of this kind of exaggeration is twofold. It can play into the Enemy's hands by attributing to him a power that he does not have. We are not dualists. We do not believe in two equal and opposite powers of good and evil, in eternal conflict that is never resolved. 'The one who is in you is greater than the one who is in the world' (I John 4:4). Os Guinness wrote:

> Too much talk of the Devil gives him too much room in people's imagination if not in their theology. It is quite true that the Devil seeks to undo God's work, but it is also true…that 'the Son of God appeared for the very purpose of undoing the devil's work'.[3]

The second danger is that of false diagnosis, and even irresponsibility. Christians often say, 'the Devil is really having a go at me this week,' when all they mean is that the office-work has been heavy, the fore-man bad-tempered, or the rates department as insensitive as to send in a big demand just before Christmas. Beware of shifting responsibility. Sometimes a week of things going wrong is God's warning signal that you need to discipline your accounts, improve your resistance to irritation, or even have a quiet evening with your wife. The familiar fact that the Enemy will *use* almost any circumstance to our spiritual disadvantage does not mean that the circumstance has a demonic root.

Resisting the Devil

Paul's letter to Colosse is written against the

background of a church's over-preoccupation with spirit powers. Gnosticism, a current thought-fashion, emphasised the influence of complicated hierarchies of supposed spirit powers. The proposed answer was a technique for people in on the secret. It invoked elaborate calendars, genealogies, rules and formulae, mystical experiences and occult meddlings which were supposed to render the spirits harmless, or obtain their co-operation.

Paul's response was quite different. He draws attention to the *total supremacy of Christ* as both God and man. In glowing words he presents the Son of God as supreme over creation (1:15–16), over time and space (1:17), over the whole Church (1:18). He is the supreme factor in the entire work of redemption (1:19–23). Then comes a magnificent assertion of his victory at the Cross. 'Having disarmed the powers and authorities, he made a public spectacle of them, triumphing over them by the cross' (2:15).

This striking metaphor is drawn from the public spectacle sometimes awarded to a victorious Roman general. Through the city he rides in triumph, surrounded by his troops, followed by carts laden with booty and then the shambling mass of defeated prisoners. It is a favourite analogy—Paul uses it again in II Corinthians 2:14–16 and Ephesians 4:7–8. The demon powers 'are shamed and exposed to public gaze; everyone can see that there is nothing to fear from these once proud soldiers.'[4]

A full-orbed view of the glory and sufficiency of Jesus: that is the need when Satan strikes. That is *faith* as the Bible presents it. The super-charismatic obsession with demons everywhere and exorcism at the drop of a hat is as unbalanced as the slightly nervous aloofness of the super-evangelical who suspects anything supernatural.

When doubts and fears arise

What should I do, then, when I suspect that a period of doubt or depression is indeed a demonic attack? There may well be a place for a firm word of authority and dismissal, spoken to your situation by a trusted senior friend or pastor. There will certainly be a place for quiet reading of the Bible and reflection on the great certainties of the faith. Peter draws a fine picture of the Christian standing up against the prowling lion of devilish attack. He is to 'stand firm in *the faith*'— that is, his confidence in the great truths of God's salvation, Satan's defeat and Christ's victory. He is to see the whole conflict in perspective, as the common experience of 'your brothers throughout the world' (I Peter 5:8–9). This is important; one of the Enemy's favourite lies is the whisper that you are alone and unique in suffering from doubt and despondency.

Paul's picture of the skilful soldier using his 'shield of faith' to quench the fiery darts flung by devilish enemies gives similar counsel. The whole point of the shield was that, unlike the other pieces of armour, it was not worn in a fixed position, but held in the hand to cover attack from any direction. Adaptability. This is when the daily, disciplined learning of the Scriptures pays off. You already know which Bible promise with which to block a particular attack. 'Faith here means the ability to apply quickly what we believe, so as to repel everything the devil attempts.'[5]

Comrades in arms

Something often forgotten in strongly individualistic evangelical circles is that Paul's whole picture of warfare is a community image. A Roman soldier fighting alone would be absurd. Roman armies moved and conquered *en masse*; their whole strategy depended upon unity, loyalty, discipline. One of the strategies of Satan is to get the doubting dismayed Christian on his own—or persuade him that he is. Yet every image of Christian advance in the New Testament is one of corporateness, which shouts aloud 'You are not on your own.'

We are members of a Church, citizens of a Kingdom, limbs of a body, worshippers in a priesthood, soldiers in an army, children of a family, living stones in a temple. Emphasis on this fact, with practical suggestions for ways to express it, is another bonus of 'renewal'. Small-group nurture, corporate prayer, joyful celebration, the expression of oneness in breaking bread, singing, hugging, helping...all of these activities help to silence Satan's whisper that the battle is too lonely to be worth continuing.

Bunyan's otherwise masterly picture of pilgrimage has a rare fault here. His own very personal experience, fortified by common Puritan thinking, encouraged the image of a brave, lonely man in solitary hand-to-hand contest with Apollyon, very occasionally meeting up for a while with Faithful, Hopeful or Evangelist, but normally pursuing his pathway alone. Significantly, after his release from prison and several years' experience of the fellowship of the Bedford Baptists, his Book II of *Pilgrim's Progress* presents an altogether different picture. Christiana sets off with her children and is soon joined by Mercy and Greatheart. Before the journey is half through, it is taking on the appearance of a walking tour rather than a pilgrimage. Before it has ended, so many people have tagged on that it looks suspiciously like a church outing, to which is added at one point what can only be described as a giant-hunt. The lonely man who once wrestled with his soul has discovered the simple

joys of church fellowship, the gentle support of family
life, and the manly companionship of many
Stouthearts and Standfasts. We all need to make the
same discoveries.

Richard Lovelace, who has carefully studied the
elements of revival and renewal throughout Christian
history, makes this crucial:

> Puritan Christians were like spiritual deep-
> sea divers, each with his or her own air line
> up to God...each one intent on private
> goals, (viewing) others only dimly through
> clouded face-plates. This happened be-
> cause the Reformers did not grasp an im-
> portant truth. *Among the most vital means
> of grace are other Christians*. Neither the
> Bible nor the sacraments will leave the shelf
> or the sanctuary to rescue a Christian who is
> too discouraged or backslidden to pray or
> worship. But a concerned brother or sister
> will do this again and again.[6]

The loneliness of leadership

A book published years ago was called *The Loneliness
of the Long-distance Runner*. This would be an appropriate title for a book about the perils of Christian
leadership. Traditional church structures, often enthusiastically encouraged by the men in the ministry,
have placed pastors in solitary positions, segregated
from the rest of the church's life by unrealistic expectations of their giftedness and performance (public
and private). My own experience in Baptist circles has
brought the observation that many men want it that
way. For the young, fresh from college, an indepen-

dent command is the epitome of success. For the more experienced, in larger churches, the idea of a lay leadership or a team of ordained men is seen as a threat. God's purpose, I am convinced, is plural leadership by people bound together in friendship and trust—not a committee representing competing interests and opinions, democratically elected like a town council of Conservatives, Socialists, Alliance and Trotskyites. Instead, the leaders should be committed to each other: sharing vision, encouraging, rebuking if necessary, warning, helping and supporting. Doubt of the most appalling kinds can nibble away at the outer edges of the life of a man who has no such support. His vision, gifts, methods, suitability for the job, confidence in the Church as an institution, confidence in himself as family bread-winner...all are undermined until he crashes. Another casualty is added to the growing list: nervous breakdown, perhaps; resignation from the pastorate; feverish preoccupation with some peripheral, exotic variant of doctrine or practice; creeping heresy, as his confidence in the Bible itself is undermined; an affair with some attractive woman in the congregation who seems to respond to his questions and cries better than the deacons— institutional isolation has claimed another victim.

Yet the antidote is available in God's provision of covenant fellowship and plural leadership. Judas' betrayal of Jesus was marginally worse than Peter's cursing denial. But what really separated the two of them was that Judas went off alone and destroyed himself whereas Peter was back in the team by Easter morning.

Notes

[1]John Bunyan, *Pilgrim's Progress*, Bk I.
[2]Martyn Lloyd-Jones, *The Christian Soldier* (Banner of Truth: Edinburgh, 1977), p 302.
[3]Os Guinness, *Doubt* (Lion Publishing: Tring, 1976), p 171.
[4]Richard Lucas, *Fullness and Freedom: the message of Colossians* (IVP: Leicester, 1980), p 110.
[5]Lloyd-Jones, *op cit*, p 305.
[6]Richard F Lovelace, *Renewal as a Way of Life* (IVP: Downers Grove, 1985), p 178.

Chapter 11

Doubting Castle and What Kept Them There

Pilgrim's Progress is an incomparable classic. Bunyan's description of Doubting Castle and what befell there is a compendium of shrewd psychology, gentle humour and spiritual insight.

The daunting episode follows a blissful time when the path pursued by Christian and Hopeful ran alongside 'the river of water of life which was pleasant and enlivening to their weary spirits'. It had done them no end of good, but, adds Bunyan drily, they were not yet at their journey's end. Beware, all pilgrims recently home from Keswick Convention, Spring Harvest and Dales Bible Week! Beware, all Christians fresh from an experience of personal renewal, or warm from the reading of some heart-lifting spiritual classic.

Off the Path: Guidance or Despair?

Things begin to go wrong quite imperceptibly. They usually do. The path becomes rough and the pilgrims get 'much discouraged because of the way'. Circumstances can have an alarming effect on spiritual awareness. Another job application turned down, an evasive look in the doctor's eyes, a day when the children have been impossible, the 'house for sale' notice ignored for 10 months: this is when faith falters and another path beckons.

A stile beside the path leads to By-Path Meadow where the going seems easier. Only as darkness falls do they realise that they are hopelessly lost. 'And now it began to rain, and thunder and lighten in a most dreadful manner; and the waters rose amain. Then Hopeful groaned in himself, saying, O that I had kept on my way.' Christian comments ruefully, 'Who would have thought that this path should lead us out of the way?' We all know the feeling! Few things are more bewildering and testing to our faith than the discovery that decisions taken with the best of intentions have led to a frightening and expensive muddle.

I once counselled an earnest young couple in missionary work whose reaction to certain pressures showed them to be temperamentally unfit for the job. Both were in depression. Where had they gone wrong? How did I account for their sense of call and their success with the mission selection board? Where was God in all this?

Another couple were unemployed and homeless as a result of obeying what they believed was God's call. Their social welfare benefits were reduced to a pittance because voluntary work for a Christian agency had somehow breached the Department of Health and Social Security regulations. When that kind of thing drags on, not for a week or two but for 16 months, the advancing tread of Giant Despair can be heard. What happened to all those Bible promises about acknowledging God in all your ways and he will direct your path?

David Watson wrote with his customary honesty about his panic and bewilderment at discovering cancer and the need for major surgery, on the brink of a year of prayerfully planned international conferences, missions and seminars. Had he imagined God's guidance when planning them? Doesn't the whole concept of divine superintendence begin to look like a chimera?

Morning finds the pilgrim pair arrested by Giant Despair 'with grim and surly voice, armed with a grievous crab-tree cudgel'. Soon he has them locked in the dungeon of Doubting Castle. There he pays them periodic visits to beat them up, but stops short of killing them. Instead, he announces that their plight is hopeless and suggests they commit suicide—helpfully offering a choice of 'knife, halter or poison'.

There is subtle counsel in all this. Satan can hurt them, but he cannot destroy them; his suggestion of suicide is as near as he can get. John Bunyan knew the consolation of the doctrine of Eternal Security, but he knew a great deal about self-induced despair as well. His autobiography is full of it. Here was a highly sensitive, over-imaginative introvert, with extraordinary creative powers not yet harnessed. From the vantage point of a later peace, he admitted that some of his fears were the sobs of self-made condemnation rather than the cries of a conscience convicted by the Spirit.

When Emotion Takes Charge

There is nothing new about emotion as a source of spiritual doubt. We have new words for it nowadays, but the Bible is full of examples. Moses was driven to distraction by the demands of administration. David was torn with love for a spoiled, malicious son. Jeremiah wished God had never called him to an unpopular ministry. Elijah swung from the manic to the depressive and wished for death, only days after a signs-and-wonders triumph. Paul reacted bitterly to attacks on his character. Peter swung between bravado and cowardice, open-handedness and exclusivism.

Os Guinness describes emotional doubt as the *coup d'état* from within. The Christian should know himself well enough to recognise when emotion's tide is rising, and what is the cause. The facts have not changed. Truth is still what it always was. Only my perception of the facts and my reaction to them have changed. It is my faith that is under fire, not the facts on which it is based. 'When faith is in danger of being cut off by an insurgent army of emotions, it panics and loses contact with the faithfulness of God.'[1]

The objectivity of God (the centre of faith) is replaced by the subjectivity of feeling. No wonder the ground shifts underfoot.

There are certain things we must grasp if emotion is not to become our master and faith its trembling servant. Feelings are involuntary. We have little control over their coming and going. That may depend on factors as varied as diet, the weather, a child's digestion, menstrual cycles, sexual appetite, the memory of a childhood experience, side-effects of a medicine, the six o'clock news, or a letter from the income-tax office—all have their effect. Emotion plays a regular confidence trick; euphoria paints the facts better, anger or depression paint them worse than they really are. The psalmist knew about it. 'Thou hast kept count of my tossings; put thou my tears in thy bottle! Are they not in thy book?' (Ps 56:8 RSV).

Those long nights, tossing and turning in bed, punching the pillow which seems to go hot and lumpy under my cheek...we know what the psalmist means. We run the mental video all night; recalling what happened, thinking of all the things we should have said, planning that stiff letter to be written in the morning. God knows about it. He counts every time you turn; he stores up your tears; he keeps a record of your fears.

But whatever you do, don't believe everything your emotions tell you. They will, if it suits them, picture your wife as another Jezebel, your boss as a second Hitler, your minister as a crooked heretic, yourself as a hopeless failure and your God as a deaf tyrant. They are wrong.

Someone says, 'I really feel that God is near.' Splendid. Make the most of it. But he is omnipresent. He is no nearer when you feel him near, and no further away when you don't. Your best prayers *may* be during that time when you really enjoy them and feel ecstatically grateful. But consider the possibility that you may please God far more when you cannot conjure up one pious emotion, but simply pray because it is the right thing to do. That is your regenerate heart speaking, moved by Word and Spirit.

And what about that chill sense that God just isn't there, and the whole Christian system is a con trick? The suspicion is desperately real to you, but it bears no relationship to the facts in heaven or earth.

C S Lewis discussed the effect of emotion on faith in one of his wartime broadcasts.

> I am not talking of moments at which any real new reasons against Christianity turn up. Those have to be faced, and that is a different matter. I am talking about moments when a mere mood rises up against it.
>
> Now faith is the art of holding onto things your reason has once accepted, in spite of your changing moods. Now that I am a Christian I do have moods in which the whole thing looks very improbable: but when I was an atheist I had moods in which Christianity looked terribly probable.
>
> That is why faith is such a necessary virtue: unless you teach your moods 'where they get off' you can never be a sound

Christian…but just a creature dithering to and fro, with its beliefs really dependent on the weather and the state of its digestion.[2]

Common Sense Prescriptions

But do you give emotion its marching orders? Not by fighting it, but by picking up a tip from the martial arts and allowing its own force and momentum to be exercised in your favour.

A village near my home town in Cleveland is troubled by periodic floods. Its stream and water meadows cannot cope with the run-off of heavy rain from the North York Moors. After two days of downpour, the muddy swirl is in the houses. Recently the local authority dug out an alternative channel, fixed a sluice gate and installed a water-wheel. Now the dangerous stream is channelled off and produces energy where once it created havoc. We can learn to do that with our emotions.

In some circumstances I find a long walk soaks up some of the emotional energy and the rest is turned into creative thought or prayer as I walk. The kind that causes that tossing on the pillow I sometimes channel by writing an angry letter in the small hours— destined for the waste-paper basket next morning.

Shortly before his operation, haunted and harried by fears, David Watson took his family to see a *Pink Panther* film. Two hours of falling around laughing redirected and exhausted the surplus agitation. Wise man. I take similar action when excessive creative work pushes me towards mild depression or the dreaded ennui. My equivalent of *Pink Panther* is a *Jeeves* book in winter or a couple of hours crewing someone's sailing dinghy in summer.

Does this sound disconcertingly unspiritual? That is intentional. Emotion sometimes does not deserve to be treated too seriously. Why give neurosis the time and attention it is bidding for? The danger is that 2 hours of so-called prayer can (in some circumstances) degenerate into 120 minutes of mental perambulation around those simpering shadows of self-pity, merely gazing at them from 20 different angles.

Of course, a turn at the Bible and a brief, disciplined time of prayer will sometimes provide the required antidote. In that case, the chosen passage should be either one that pours out the emotion once and for all to God, or one that focuses the mind on the unchanging reality of the Almighty. Psalm 73 very usefully does both. Prayer in these circumstances should be occupied with the Lord rather than lengthy confession. The advent of beautiful and memorable worship songs on cassette tapes has reintroduced in a new form the well tried comfort and stimulus of Word and music combined, the one bringing objective truth and the other catching subjective mood.

Many Christians, I suspect, have their favourite spiritual classics—well-worn books whose very familiarity is a solace. Immerse yourself in one of those, and you begin to put agitation in its place simply by changing the subject and evoking happy memories. If you have the words almost by heart, all the better; your mind moves freely over the meaning rather than concentrating on the precise words. My own list, always by me, is an odd assortment from different centuries. It includes John Bunyan's *Grace Abounding to the Chief of Sinners*, John Newton's *Letters*, G K Chesterton's *The Everlasting Man*, A W Pink's *The Sovereignty of God*, a miscellany of C S Lewis, and a compendium of collects from the Alternative Service Book of the Church of England. What they, and others, have in common is their ability to lift me out of myself and turn my attention to God and his ways. Incidentally, they give me a 'feeling' too: the sensation of drinking cold water in the desert.

Unashamed humanity

Inner turmoil may be used as an enemy of our best interests, but emotion *per se* is not a thing to be ashamed of. I am subjective because I am human. The Son of God took our humanity and he *felt*. He wept. He was angry. He was sarcastic. He laughed (the parables and sayings are full of impish humour).

Charismatic renewal has helped to make emotion respectable again. We Anglo Saxons with our stiff upper lips had entered into a conspiracy of silence about emotion. Renewal has knocked the lid off and liberated thousands of Christians from the idea that you have to leave both your limbs and your feelings behind when you go to church.

Unfortunately it is not all gain. Too many contemporary Christians have made emotion the largest part of Christianity. The presence of God becomes wholly identified with elation. The power of the Holy Spirit is exclusively identified with excitement. This is dangerous, for as we have noted, feelings by their very nature are cyclic, recurrent, erratic. The Christian who associates emotion's coming with God's arrival may identify its going with his departure. But it is not so.

The common experience of early joy at conversion simply will not and cannot last. C S Lewis somewhere compares it to the high tide that gets a ship into dry dock; the real repair job gets under way when the water has served its purpose and dropped again. When the tide ebbs, the convert will begin to discover just how much (or little) theology, Bible knowledge and supportive facts he has taken aboard. If he has taken on nothing, Giant Despair's grievous crab-tree cudgel will inflict some nasty bruises.

Back on Course

Sailing is a splendid sport. I especially enjoy that breathless moment when, with sails hoisted, ropes furled, tide tugging at the centre-board, wind clapping the sails, I am ready to take control. Cast off the mooring. With one hand pull in the mainsail sheet. With the other, grasp the tiller firmly and push it over. Suddenly, almost unbelievably, confusion gives way to purposeful power and the boat surges forward on course. As before, wind, tide, rudder and keel are all reacting upon one another. But now they do what I want them to do. There is no feeling quite like it.

Paul speaks of bringing every wilful thought under the control of Christ. The wild wind of emotion can be channelled into usefulness and purpose, direction and energy...once we have the measure of it, learn something of its ways, and establish whose hand is on the tiller. When I first learned to sail, on a gusty tidal Essex backwater, a seasoned yachtsman sat beside me, his hand over mine on the tiller. Jesus Christ does that for us, and never takes his hand off as long as we invite him to keep it on.

Notes

[1]Os Guinness, *Doubt* (Lion Publishing: Tring, 1976), p 127.
[2]C S Lewis, broadcast talks, published 1952 as *Mere Christianity* (Collins/Fount: London, 1981 reprint), p 122.

Chapter 12

Doubting Castle and the Way Out

We have left the pilgrims in Doubting Castle for a long time, but so did John Bunyan: four days to be exact. During that time they did a lot of talking. Bunyan knew about the dynamics of small-group sharing; it was his observation of devout housewives on their sunny doorsteps in Bedford discussing their souls that first set him on the Christian pilgrimage.

> In one of the streets of that town, I came where there were three or four poor women, sitting at a door in the sun and talking about the things of God...I heard, but I understood not, for they were far above, out of my reach. Methought they spoke as if joy did make them speak, they spoke with such pleasantness of Scripture language and such appearance of grace that they were to me as if they had found a new world.[1]

Thousands of Christians today are finding the same in housegroups, nurture cells and preparation classes around the country.

The pilgrims' discussion rehearsed some of the solid reasons why doubt and despair should not have its way. In very Puritan fashion they revolve around two issues: the utter reliability of God's Word and the high dignity of being a child of God. 'Let us consider what the Lord of the country to which we are going hath said' suggests Hopeful. Precisely. The best antidote to creeping doubt is the Word of God—towering, objective, divine—speaking to our circumstances but not dependent upon them, touching our emotions, but not changed by them. That means more than assorted texts: rather, it means the wide, deep sense of the whole sweep of Scripture that only comes by imbibing it day by day before the crisis comes. A knowledge like that is not restricted to people who have read it since childhood. I have talked to converts of 18 months' standing who already have a broad grasp of the whole biblical message. It is Spirit-taught and does not depend on the same principles as secular knowledge.

Not Alone

Hopeful had another cheering thought: 'Others, so far as I can understand, have been taken by Giant Despair as well as we, and yet have escaped out of his hands.' That is a peculiarly consoling reflection; others as well as we. Satan often whispers the suggestion of loneliness and oddity. You may well be the only Christian in your hall of residence (factory, office, household). Might you not be mistaken, and the whole Christian life a fallacy? Almost as bad is to know several other believers, but to imagine yourself unique in having doubts, reservations or a spiritual 'down'. They never feel like this, you suspect.

Christian fellowship shares the conflict with those who are alive; Christian biography passes on the experience of those who once lived. No Christian should be so ignorant of the discoveries of fellow Christians that he imagines himself alone.

The Biblical Key

At length the pilgrims graduate from talking to each other and begin to talk with God. The result is remarkable. With a start of surprise, Christian remembers something.

> What a fool I am, thus to lie in a stinking
> dungeon when I may as well walk at liberty.
> I have a key in my bosom called Promise,
> that will, I am persuaded, open any lock in
> Doubting Castle.

The key represents, not simply the Word of God, but *the believer's ability to use it and apply it*. Bunyan is back to a favourite theme which surfaces every few pages of *Pilgrim's Progress, Grace Abounding* and *The Holy War*. The Bible is full of promises which bring God's objective Word to bear on the Christian's subjective experience. Bunyan's autobiography spells out that lesson more than any other.

> And now I began to look into the Bible with
> new eyes; and especially the epistles of the
> apostle Paul were sweet and pleasant to
> me...Especially the word *faith* put me to it:
> I questioned whether I had any faith or
> no...Oh, many a pull hath my heart had
> with Satan for that blessed sixth of
> John...he pulled and I pulled but, God be
> praised, I got the better of him.[2]

(The reference is to John 6:37: 'All that the Father gives me will come to me, and whoever comes to me I will never drive away.')

That key, tucked into Christian's inside pocket all

the time, unlocks every door, once he actually uses it. The pilgrims make a run for it. Giant Despair pursues them, but not for long. Once out of the shadow of the castle, he falls down in one of his periodic fits. For, as a child once gravely explained to me in a Sunday school essay, Giant Despair is allergic to sunshine.

Believing the Word of God

The starting-point of Bible application is, of course, *belief* in the Bible. By that I mean not merely belief in its helpfulness and wholesomeness, but acceptance of its authority and commitment to its truth. It can be put simply and bluntly. The Bible is totally and uniquely true because it records what God has said in the way he chose to say it. That is what Jesus Christ believed, and the Christian, by definition, is a follower of Jesus Christ. So the believer approaches the Bible in a unique way. No religious book, however inspiring, has this authority. No church leader, however dynamic, has this kind of clout. No contemporary word of prophecy, revelation, commentary or counsel, can bring this certainty. No experience, however authentic, can bring this objectivity.

Herein lurks an emotive issue. Evangelicals today are polarising into two groups. The first bitterly condemns the second, and the second derisively dismisses the first. What is involved in believing the Bible?

Some 'reformed' Christians (not all) see contemporary claims for the exercise of spiritual gifts (such as prophecy, words of knowledge, discernment) as a frontal attack on the completeness and sufficiency of Scripture. Take your pick, they seem to say. Choose an inspired, infallible Bible, or choose a contemporary work of the Spirit. You cannot have both.

Meanwhile, some 'charismatic' Christians (not all)

regard the objective truth of the Bible as rather dull stuff compared with the thrilling experience of prophecy and divine guidance. The reading and study of the Bible is put in second place to subjective experience. After the anecdote-sharing and 'ministry' at the housegroup, there *might* be time for God's Word, but first things first!

The resulting clash is one of today's tragedies. It is confidence in God's Word that suffers, in both parties. Those who, in the name of an infallible Bible, suspect anything that moves, are in danger of imprisoning Scripture in a cage of orthodoxy and nostalgia. They are saying, 'Yes I believe with all my heart in an inspired Bible picture of the Early Church. But of course it is not for us. *Today's* Church looks, not to the everyday intervention of the Holy Spirit but to the pages of the Bible. Instead of apostles we have Epistles. Instead of words of knowledge we have knowledge of the Word. Instead of prophecy we have theology.'

Meanwhile, those who, in the name of spiritual immediacy, suspect anything that is fixed or firm, drift ever further away from the moorings of what God has already said and done. The Bible becomes, not their guiding light, but a torch sometimes switched on when they occasionally stop to regain their breath. With it, they look hurriedly around for some scriptural text (however stretched) to justify their most recent experiment, experience or excitement.

The key, meanwhile, nestles in an inside pocket, unused by either party. One group is content to keep it there, and make ringing declarations about the pure metal from which it is made. The other leaves it there, because it is more fun to try speaking words of faith to the locked door in the hope that it will swing open miraculously.

Denying the Word of God

In Bunyan's time, believing the Bible to be true was no problem. Competing religious systems differed in emphasis and interpretation, but no one doubted its essential truth. That is no longer so. A century-and-a-half of liberal theology and scholarly 'criticism' has left the modern pilgrim uncertain about the very authority of his faith. Liberal theology, if taken mercilessly to its logical conclusion, offers a *different Bible*. Scripture is presented, not as God's Word to people, but as people's words about God. The liberal Bible is offered for our examination and judgement. But this is not at all the way in which the Bible offers itself. It invites us (indeed commands us) to stand under its judgement and experience the impact of its truth. It points us to Jesus—the Jesus of its own pages, not Jesus the social reformer or the apocalyptic dreamer or the socialist-pacifist or the gentle rabbi, or the revolutionary. It offers the divine-human Son of God, who died to break sin's consequences, left the tomb empty, and gives new life by his Spirit.

Defining the Word of God

Because of this controversy, Christians have found it necessary to introduce definitions to safeguard their commitment to the Bible. Phrases such as *verbal infallibility, plenary inspiration*, and (most recently) *inerrancy* have been introduced. What is the believer to make of this? Is it an essence of faith in the Bible to affirm that every word is true? Literally true? Historically true? Scientifically true? What about literary style in the Bible? In what sense is poetry 'true'? What about symbols in the Bible? What is symbolic and what is not? Should I settle for a literal Adam but a symbolic fruit tree? A minister who invited me to preach in his pulpit and then had uneasy second thoughts asked me anxiously whether I believed that a 1,000-year Millennium would follow a war between Russia and America fought out in northern Israel, and that during the Millennium lions would become vegetarian. Does belief in the Bible require all that? Is hesitation about that kind of thing a form of unbelief that weakens my foundation of faith?

Emotional Blackmail

These are not theoretical quibbles. The Christian who asks questions may well find himself pressurised from opposite angles, subjected to some harassment that is a form of emotional blackmail. If he hesitates or demurs, one party will despise him as an ignoramus, and the other will accuse him of heresy.

At this point it is attitude, not definition, that is crucial. Am I amongst those who 'tremble at the words of God' (Ezra 9:4)? Do I approach the reading of the Bible as if I were indeed approaching God? I must be reverent, receptive, submissive.

'May my cry come before you, O Lord; give me understanding according to your word' (Ps 119:169). In such an attitude, I must reject the basic approach of so-called modern scholarly criticism. This is not because I am an obscurantist who despises scholarship. (I am happily aware that much scholarship is in fact favourable to a very reverent approach to the Bible.) Rather, I have made a decision. My soul's welfare needs a firmer foundation than the shifting sand of scholarly opinion which, after all, is noted for its changing trends and theories. I am not fooled by sophistries that invite me to choose between an empty cave 2,000 years ago or a living Christ experienced today. The Bible poses no such alternative; it offers me the Christ who left the tomb empty 2,000 years ago and therefore can come to me in transforming power today. Slyly asked to agree that the *meaning* of the Bible (the thrust of the message) is more vital than the mere *words* (black marks on white paper), I assert that my God is perfectly capable of saying what he means.

Words are capable of carrying exact meaning. God has chosen to make himself known in words. The words he chose to use are preserved in the Bible. Jesus says so, and he is my Lord.

However, we must enter another caveat at this point. The purpose of words such as 'inerrant' and 'infallible' is not simply to freeze the living truth of God's Word into a set formula which then provides a statement to cover every contingency. The Bible is not a book of rules. It is not even an indexed compendium of systematic theology, with sections on God, man, salvation and ecclesiology, like those useful volumes which used to be called Bodies of Divinity.

The story of the living God (his words and deeds for our salvation) cannot be turned into a still photograph to be framed and hung upon the wall. God is known by his deeds—and his words explain his deeds. That fact certainly underlines how necessary is an inerrant Bible. For if the words that describe his deeds are not reliable words, then we have no certainty about the deeds, and no reliable explanation of what they mean! Knowing God by his actions becomes a mere pious guessing-game.

Yet at the same time the whole emphasis is one of life, not mere flat statement. God's Word does not merely inform; it acts upon us and works within us. 'Our gospel came to you not simply with words, but also with power, with the Holy Spirit and with deep conviction' (I Thess 1:5).

A modern Baptist writer thus suggests that definitions of Bible inerrancy and explanations of its inspiration fall short of the essential thrust:

> Evangelicals have been so taken up with the debate about Scripture, its inerrancy or otherwise, the nature of its inspiration, its historical reliablity, etc, that they are in danger of missing the point. It is the function of the Scripture, not its form, which is of crucial importance.[3]

In other words, what it *is* only has full meaning in what it *does*. Paul emphasises both in his famous words to Timothy (II Tim 3:16–17): *what it is*—'all Scripture is God-breathed'; *what it does*—'...and is useful for teaching, rebuking, correcting and training in righteouness'. Two historical events which evangelicals love to recall illustrate this, but their full significance is often missed.

Consider the clash between Jesus and the Pharisees. It was not a conflict between belief and disbelief in the written Word of God. Both believed the Bible. The Pharisees were fundamentalists to a man. Yet somehow they failed to grasp either its message or its purpose. Jesus put his finger on it:

> You diligently study the Scriptures because you think that by them you possess eternal life. These are the Scriptures that testify about me, yet you refuse to come to me to have life.
>
> (John 5:39)

They imagined that their mere possession of the sacred scrolls somehow gave them a different position with God. They had not grasped that the Bible is an invitation to search for Christ, not a celebration of ownership. In the words of John Stott: 'They became so engrossed in the *words* that they lost sight of the *truth*…They were not concerned about the *message* of Scripture but only about *meanings*.'[4]

The second example is the Protestant Reformation. Catholics, in fact, firmly believed the Bible.

> The difference between Martin Luther and his Catholic opponents was not that he knew the Bible and they did not. The crucial difference was that to Luther the Bible had become a place where he encountered Christ and knew that he had been justified by faith in him. No longer was it a textbook to be quoted along with other textbooks to prove a point. It was a means of grace, a place where he dealt with Christ and Christ dealt with him through his word.[5]

To believe the Bible, therefore, is not simply to say 'This is true', but to say, 'This is happening.' My point is that 'doubts' about the Bible, which can often attack when for some other reason the Christian is discouraged, dismayed or even disobedient, are not resolved by mentally flogging oneself for daring to have difficulties with some of its statements and stories. 'What am I willing to let it do to me?' must be the question posed and honestly answered.

Does this mean that the starting-place of faith is a definition and understanding of biblical inspiration? Must I resolve all those problems about curses in the Psalms, massacres in the Book of Joshua and scientific puzzles in the Book of Genesis, before my faith has any foundation? No. Faith's starting-place is commitment to Christ.

While in Galilee Jesus once said:

> You diligently study the Scriptures...that testify about me...If you believed Moses, you would believe me, for he wrote about me. But since you do not believe what he wrote, how are you going to believe what I say?
>
> (John 5:39–47)

In a book which itself is full of scholarship, John Wenham argues like this:

> Christians unsure about the status of the Bible have been caught in a vicious circle: any satisfactory doctrine of the Bible must be based on the teaching of the Bible, but the teaching of the Bible is itself suspect. The way out of this dilemma is to recognise that *belief in the Bible comes from faith in Christ, and not vice versa...*
>
> A convert from a non-Christian religion or from modern secular society seldom arrives at the decisive moment of faith with a view of biblical inspiration already formulated in his mind. His quest is a wrestling with the Christ portrayed in the New Testament and witnessed to by Christians. As he progresses in his search, the Gospels seem to him more and more to have the ring of truth. At last he comes to the moment when he says 'Lord I believe.' He has arrived at faith with a conviction about the basic truth of the New Testament witness to Christ, but

without necessarily any clear beliefs about
the truth or falsity of many details or about
the status of the Bible as a whole.[6]

This is obviously true and illustrations of it are
numerous in the experience of those who are actually
sharing Christ with others in school, college, factory,
housegroup, evangelistic mission. Unfortunately,
with the best of motives, some preachers and church
leaders want to reverse the order, and claim that until
we get people to say, 'Yes, Jonah was swallowed by a
whale; the water of the Red Sea stood up like a wall;
there were elephants and kangaroos in Noah's ark;
and the universe was made in 6 days of 24 hours,' we
cannot introduce them to the Son of God. Their laud-
able commitment to the whole Bible (which I share) is
intermingled with an understandable nostalgia for the
days of Martin Luther, John Bunyan and D L Moody.
But it just won't do. It is Jesus Christ who saves, not
theories—however correct—about the Bible's authority...not even theories about the Atonement:
Jesus Christ himself, revealed to the human heart by
the Holy Spirit.

For this reason, *what Jesus says about the Bible* is
the Christian's starting-place. The believer should not
feel bullied into making definitive statements about
how many hours God may have taken to create the
universe, or whether the tree of life had literal bark
and leaves. What Jesus draws from the early Genesis
accounts is truth, such as the sanctity and security of
marriage (Matt 19:3-9) and the fact that Satan has
always been a liar (John 8:44).

This is exactly in accord with the rest of the Bible's
use of that passage, whether in Old or New Testament. The psalmist draws a fundamental truth about
man's place in God's world (Ps 8). The apostle Paul

builds a profound argument on the consequences of Adam's disobedience and Christ's obedience (Rom 5:12–17).

This is the thinking behind the suggested formula, 'Scripture is true and factual in all it *asserts*.' If it asserts a historical fact in the language of historical narrative, then what it asserts is historically true and factual. But if it speaks in what is obviously the language of poetry, symbolism or apocalypse, then it is not what it *says* (the literal words) but what it *asserts* (the truth picturesquely expressed) that is binding upon the believing reader.

To point this out is not to dodge infallibility. But to say *infallible* is not quite enough. What do the words *mean*? What do all those letters, reports, commands, poems, parables and allegories tell me? Faith takes its stand on the Scripture. It vows, 'I will receive what it means, I will believe what it asserts, and with God's help I will do what it requires.'

Getting Hold of the Key

Once Christ has saved me then, without doubt, I will be brought sooner or later to an understanding of the power and authority of the Bible, and will surrender increasingly to its claims. Growing knowledge of what it says, growing experience of how it works, growing discovery of its amazing relevance and all-encompassing scope: this is the path to confidence in biblical authority. Equipped with a growing knowledge of the Bible, the modern pilgrim will find, like Bunyan's Christian, that he has a key in his inside pocket that can unlock any door and effect his release from Doubting Castle.

Working at it

There is no short cut. Effort is required, Richard Lovelace, analysing the invariable features of spiritual renewal, warns: 'The Christian who wants to encounter God without listening to what he has to say may remain in the condition of a smiling, subliterate and disobedient two year old.'[7]

To get to know the Bible takes discipline, especially the discipline of time. A Scripture reading with comment and ideas for prayer can be fitted into most people's day. I know scores of people who read their Bibles on commuter trains to work. An outstanding member of parliament assured me that he does his Bible reading on the London Underground. Mothers with small children have discovered the priceless asset of the cassette player. Organisations such as Scripture Union and Every Day With Jesus provide material for every age and class. Even a surprisingly small daily reading, if a scheme is followed, can cover the text of the Bible in one year.

Hard to fit it in? I reckon that the time required for both of these exercises is equivalent to the average person's use of a daily newspaper, the weekly television programme details and a monthly hobby journal or professional magazine.

Knowing and understanding

Knowledge is not enough. How do I *understand*? The Author of the Book stands ready to interpret it for me. The Holy Spirit, who inspired its writing, brings it to light in the understanding of the reader. It is this that makes the reading of the Bible totally different from any other kind of reading. It really is (or rather can be) an encounter with the living God in which the

Spirit in me becomes his own Interpreter, answering to the Spirit in the written Word.

> The Spirit searches all things, even the deep things of God…no one knows the thoughts of God except the Spirit of God…We have…received…the Spirit who is from God, that we may understand what God has freely given us.
>
> (I Cor 2:10–13)

> He who has an ear, let him hear what the Spirit says…
>
> (Rev 2:7)

The qualification for reading and understanding is not mental or academic: it is nothing to do with how many O-levels I have, or whether I am the reading type. Addressing a dinner in the members' dining room of the House of Commons once, I was asked whether it was not too much to expect people who are not 'bookish types' to read and understand the Bible. I replied that this was completely irrelevant. The Bible is not a bookish kind of book; it is a living message from God, designed for listeners and learners, not scholars. On my way there I had passed several signposts and had used several instruction boards on the London Underground. So had many other people, not particularly good readers. What we all needed was information, instruction and direction, and that's what we were given. This is what the Bible gives us, and the way to understand it and benefit from it is simply to be willing to follow.

Benefits of a stocked mind

The Christian who stocks his mind with Bible truth is laying up provision for days when faith will be tested. Truth is learned in its original context—Joseph's bad treatment in Egypt, Elijah's surrender to depression, David's mishandling of his family, Paul's shipwreck, Timothy's nervousness, etc. It leaps to life later when their context becomes ours in the interplay of life's circumstances. Solid doctrine is imbibed as an interesting study in, say, the holiness of God, the meaning of redemption, the high priestly office of Jesus. Much later, perhaps, it becomes vividly applicable to some situation of weakness, temptation, failure or fear. The believer with a stocked mind does not have to thumb through a topical index to find an appropriate verse; he already knows his way around the library of truth.

I once met a Chinese Christian fresh from 11 years in prison. The Red Guards had ransacked his home, piled up a bonfire of his furniture and thrown his beloved chain-reference Bible onto the fire before dragging him away to prison. After his release some local official wished to make amends. My friend was encouraged to search through a huge warehouse of confiscated property for anything that might be his. He did so without the slightest expectation and, to his amazement, literally stumbled over his Bible, its cover charred but its pages intact. He stood in tears, turning it over in his hands and thanking God.

The real miracle is not in the unimaginable sequence of events that somehow brought that man and his Bible together again. Rather, it is the fact that for those long years they had never really been parted. He could say with the psalmist, 'I have hidden your word in my heart' (Ps 119:11).

That man could enthral those who met him with story after story of the power of that Word, read long before and partly memorised, as it was mentally recalled and applied in the chill hours of solitary confinement, the deafening days of verbal abuse and brainwashing, the wearying weeks of forced labour, the crawling years when the accuser whispered to him that he was forgotten. He had the key in his bosom all the time.

> Then said Hopeful, that's good news, good brother. Pluck it out of thy bosom and try. Then Christian pulled it out of his bosom, and began to try at the dungeon door, whose bolt (as he turned the key) gave back, the door flew open with ease, and Christian and Hopeful both came out... Then they went on, and came to the King's highway, and so were safe, for they were out of the jurisdiction of Giant Despair.

Notes

[1]John Bunyan, *Grace Abounding to the Chief of Sinners*.
[2]*ibid*.
[3]Nigel Wright, *The Radical Kingdom* (Kingsway: Eastbourne, 1986), p 14.
[4]John Stott, *Christ the Controversialist* (Tyndale: Leicester, 1970), p 97. The whole of chapters 2 and 3 present a brilliant exposition of this point, and of what believing in the Bible entails.
[5]Nigel Wright, *op cit*, p 14.
[6]John Wenham, *Christ and the Bible* (Tyndale Press: Leicester, 1972), pp 9–10.

[7]Richard Lovelace, *Dynamics of Spiritual Life* (Paternoster Press: Exeter, 1979), p 282.

Chapter 13

Invitation to Faith

This has been a book about doubt. I would much rather have written one about faith. After all, believing is a much more enjoyable and fruitful exercise than doubting. A friend with whom I shared my intention to write the book urged me to encourage 'positive, aggressive, expectant *faith*'. I wish to do so. We are living in a day when God invites us to move on and move out with him, supremely confident that what God has promised, he is able to perform (Rom 4:21 AV). Far too many arguments and discussions, even amongst evangelical Christians, nowadays revolve around the fact that we have brought hesitant unbelief to a fine art.

And yet...Abraham, father-figure and personification of faith, had his doubts that were not the contradiction of faith but part of the genuine struggle to believe. And at the awesome centre of the Christian's whole hope and trust is a cry from darkness beyond our ken, in words on which we hesitate to comment and must permit to echo in all their stark simplicity: 'My God, my God, why have you forsaken me?'

'Why?' and 'Why not?' are words of faith—or at any rate, they need not be words of unbelief. They may be the words of someone moving towards a faith which can have no hope of reality until at least some of the questions have been answered. They may be the words of someone who has long believed, but now finds his faith savagely attacked or surreptitiously undermined. The Devil can confront our faith as a polished rationalist who asks 'If...', a raged lion who roars 'No', an angel of light who says 'Therefore', or a serpent who hisses 'Has God really said?'

Faith has to have some starting-place. Faith in God can only begin with what God says about himself otherwise it is indistinguishable from wishful thinking. In perhaps the greatest chapter on faith in the whole Bible, the writer begins there:

> Faith is being sure of what we hope for and certain of what we do not see...Without faith it is impossible to please God, because anyone who comes to him must believe that he exists and that he rewards those who earnestly seek him.
>
> (Heb 11:1, 6)

Foundations of Faith

Exactly what is involved in believing? Clearly there must be *mental assent*. 'Yes, that seems reasonable enough. I can put an assenting tick beside that.' To say that, there must be a certain amount of information. 'This is what I am required to believe? Very well, at least I know the score.' For most people that requires a certain amount of apologetic and explanation. Christians are expected to possess enough to give a good reason to anyone who asks *why* we believe (not only *what*); so the New Testament assures us (I Peter 3:15).

The Struggle for Faith

But there is more to it than this. *Truth about God* is what we are invited to. Not trust in faith as a technique or an exercise or a way of life, but trust in God is what beckons us. We have seen how some of the Faith Formulae fail to grasp that vital point. That does not come easy. Spiritual truth, the facts about God, absolute standards, are not in the same dimension as geography, mathematics or the working of a computer.

> No eye has seen, no ear has heard, no mind has conceived what God has prepared for those who love him—but God has revealed it to us by his Spirit...The man without the Spirit does not accept the things that come from the Spirit of God, for they are foolishness to him and he cannot understand them, because they are spiritually discerned.
>
> (I Cor 2:9–10, 14)

The response of faith to truth has a more secure basis than the fact that a book was well written, a sermon particularly eloquent or a friend extra persuasive! God is at work in this!

That is why our pious ancestors spoke of God's 'irresistible grace' in calling us to faith; a concept which modern people (even modern Christians) find very uncomfortable, if not downright offensive. Yet our experience tells us it is so. We come, ultimately, because God calls us with a call that overcomes our resistance. He does not coerce us, but he most certainly persuades us so that we 'come most freely, being made willing by his grace'.[1]

In a deeply moving passage, C S Lewis describes how that persistent pleading that will not take 'No' for an answer eventually prevailed with him.

> You must picture me alone in that room at Magdalen, night after night, feeling, whenever my mind lifted for a second from my work, the steady, unrelenting approach

of Him whom I so earnestly designed not to meet...In the Trinity Term of 1929 I gave in, and admitted that God was God... perhaps, that night, the most dejected and reluctant convert in all England...The Prodigal Son at least walked home on his own feet. But who can duly adore that love which will open the high gates to a prodigal who is brought in kicking, struggling, resentful and darting his eyes in every direction for a chance to escape?...The hardness of God is kinder than the softness of men, and His compulsion is our liberation.[2]

A very different type of Christian, the Victorian Charles Spurgeon, records the same experience. In his case he imagined that he was seeking God for months, yet found it impossible to believe. One morning, prevented by a snow blizzard from attending his usual church, he slipped into the nearest Primitive Methodist Chapel. The snow that kept him from his own church kept the minister from this one, and the congregation had to make do with an ill-equipped and unprepared lay preacher who was obliged to stick to his text for the simple reason that he had little else to say.

The text was from Isaiah: 'Look unto me and be ye saved, all the ends of the earth.' In a simple, almost crude way he spent about 10 minutes explaining that there was nowhere else to look. Then, having exhausted his theme, he looked around for a suitable conclusion, and caught the eye of young Charles, a stranger sitting alone.

Just fixing his eye on me as if he knew all my heart, he said, 'Young man you look very miserable—and you always will be miserable—miserable in life and miserable in death, if you don't obey my text. Young man, look to Jesus Christ. Look! Look! Look! You have nothing to do but look and live.' I saw at once. Oh! I looked until I could almost have looked my eyes away. There and then the cloud was gone, the darkness had rolled away...I thought I could dance all the way home.[3]

Must I then sit and wait for it to strike me, like lightning, or influenza, or falling in love? No, for faith is not a feeling but an attitude that springs from a decision. In Lewis's words, I must let God be God. Do I *want* to believe? Many do not. It is too awkward, too demanding. Have I grasped what the alternative is?

We accept man's testimony, but God's testimony is greater because it is the testimony of God, which he has given about his Son... Anyone who does not believe God has made him out to be a liar.

(I John 5:9–10)

Am I prepared to adjust my attitudes? Will passing opinions (the 'assured results of modern scholarship' that change as often as the calendar year, the cultural opinions and trends that change almost as often as the weather forecast) count with me more than what God has said, and his people have proved? Shall I allow shifting circumstances and cyclic emotions a louder voice in my life than the 'still small voice' of God that remains unchanged in the message it whispers? Am I prepared to say that I don't understand what God is doing just at present, but I would rather have his sometimes mysterious hand on the tiller than leave the ship of my life unsteered in the storm?

God himself is the Giver of faith

But he does not give it in an arbitrary unpredictable fashion. He who gives faith also gives us the capacity for belief, incentives to believe, and aids to faith. Most of all he has given the Bible. Because it comes from him, it has the ability to stir up faith within us. 'Faith comes by hearing, and hearing by the word of God' (Rom 10:17 AV). We may imagine the reverse process: 'If I could only believe the Bible, I would read it.' But God says, 'Read the Bible, and you will find yourself believing it' (exactly what Lewis and Spurgeon were doing prior to their conversion).

Faith comes to focus in commitment

Sooner or later I am faced with the poser, 'What shall I *do* with this invitation to believe?' There is only one answer, expressed in a hundred ways. Don't just read the destination on the front of the bus...climb on. Don't just peer at Jesus walking on the water...step out of the boat. Don't just talk about learning to drive...put yourself in the hands of the instructor. Don't just admire the Bread of Life and analyse its calorific value...eat it. That deliberate decision for commitment will have to be made, not only in the matter of conversion, but in the ceaseless pressures, questions and choices of life, as repeated steps of faith are taken.

Faith has to be tested

There is no other way. An athlete will not prepare his muscles for the Olympics by nursing them and keeping them inactive, but by challenging them and stretching them in constant challenge and practice. The learner-driver will never develop his latent skill by only ever driving on empty country lanes; he has to plunge into the frightening test of the heavy traffic, the unpredictable pedestrian, the changing lights and the hill starts. As the apostle Peter says, faith is more valuable than gold, and like gold, it can only be purified by fire. The haunting spectre of doubt, the cold chill of disappointed hope, the prayer that sometimes seems to bounce back from the ceiling, the question that has no immediate answer...these are sometimes the very processes which give the faith-athlete muscle, and equip the believer-driver to get somewhere on his journey.

And at the starting-point of the race, at every place along its route, and waiting to greet us at the winning-post is Jesus, the Author and Perfector of our faith: the One on whom faith depends from start to finish.

Notes

[1]Westminster Confession XII:1.
[2]C S Lewis, *Surprised by Joy* (Collins/Fontana: London, 1976 reprint), pp 182–83.
[3]C H Spurgeon, *The Early Years* (Banner of Truth: Edinburgh, 1962), pp 88–89.

When Christians Fail

by Michael A Apichella

Apparent failure is hard to accept. Westerners, it seems, must only fail in private. Failure is vice, success is virtue, and winning the name of the game.

How often do we as Christians adopt the world's standards, focus on the winners, turn away from the losers? How often do we condemn ourselves if we fail in our job, our exams, our spiritual disciplines? Why does God allow us to stumble? In despair, can we see a way forward?

Michael Apichella offers encouragement to 'Christians who must endure the stinging nettles of life – whether through a broken marriage, humiliation at work, failed health, a fruitless ministry, or any of a hundred other possible heartbreaks. These are painful and lonely experiences, but our failures needn't destroy us.' Drawing on biblical and contemporary examples, he offers a way of understanding and learning from our failures.

Michael Apichella works freelance for the BBC. He says of himself that he is well acquainted with failure, but that in Christ he can go forward in hope.

192pp   £2.50

Dark Glasses

Sex, poetry, the media and quite a bit else

Edited by Steve Shaw and Sue Plater

Why should the thorny subjects so often be swept under the carpet? Isn't it time the Church started talking, thinking, and acting on contemporary issues?

Steve Shaw and Sue Plater have collected a series of essays with questions and responses for discussion starters. Homosexuality, the theatre, materialism, feminism, pornography, rock music – all these and many other subjects come under thoughtful scrutiny by a well known panel of writers including Pip Wilson, Martin Wroe, Nigel Forde, Stewart Henderson and Viv Faull.

An indispensable book for youth and their leaders, for new Christians, for any who are asking questions.

Co-published with the Greenbelt Arts Festival

192pp   £3.95

God's Mission:
Healing the Nations

by Dr David Burnett

God's healing: the streams of the water of life. Christians are the messengers carrying that healing mission from God: calming, reconciling, easing conflict. Who can ignore such a commission from God? It is not a soft option, says Dr Burnett, but a command we are challenged to obey.

God's Mission: Healing the Nations explores the vision of mission throughout the ages. Dr Burnett examines the divergences in concept and understanding lucidly and with compassion — challenging us to realise that mission is both a calling and a privilege which none of us can afford to turn away from.

Discussion questions, suggested readings and an extensive booklist are practical aids in pursuing the topic beyond the printed page.

David Burnett is Principal of the Missionary Orientation Centre at the WEC International headquarters at Bulstrode in Buckinghamshire. He has served as a missionary in India, and he and his wife, Anne, have two children.

Co-published with the Evangelical Missionary Alliance and Send the Light Books.

256pp   £2.75

Characters Around the Cross

by the Rev Tom Houston

The Cross of Jesus, leading to the Resurrection, imposes meaning upon the inherently tragic nature of life. Tom Houston, in this fascinating and often moving book, leads us through the events and emotions surrounding the Crucifixion.

Peter, Pilate, the crowds who demanded Christ's death, Mary Magadalene — experience the events with them; gain insight into their motives, their love, their grief.

'Not only do the market-places, courtrooms, streets and shrines take on a new earthly reality, but the writings of their day bear a striking relevance to our own world.' *Today*, April, 1986

The Rev Tom Houston, formerly Executive Director of the British and Foreign Bible Society, is now President of World Vision International.

160pp £1.95

The Urban Christian

by Raymond Bakke with Jim Hart

Foreword by Bishop David Sheppard

How do we go about caring for people in the desperate and deprived areas of today's inner cities? Ray Bakke provides fresh answers – answers that are based on practical experience, notably free from academic and ecclesiastical jargon. He sets inner-city Christian work firmly into its global context and shows how the Church can rise above its urban malaise to discover God's rich resources.

> 'It should be required reading for all Christians in Britain…. The book is an essential supplement to *Faith in the City*, for it clothes the bones of theory with the flesh of theology, practicality and a global perspective.'
>
> *Third Way*

Dr Ray Bakke has lived and worked in inner-city Chicago for more than twenty years. He is now Professor of Ministry at Northern Baptist Theological Seminary in Illinois.

Co-published with ECUM

216pp   £4.95